1 Introduction

Shamanism is the oldest religion on the planet! In terms of human existence, it predates current day organized religions by tens of thousands of years. European cave paintings and carvings showing shaman date from the Paleolithic era. Graves of shaman 12,000-year-old and older have been discovered in Israel and the Czech Republic.

In this book, we will explore shaman and shamanism in Tibet, Nepal, Mongolia and modern-day South Korea. We look at Bon, the religion that came after shamanism in that part of the world and incorporated shamanism and shamanic traditions into itself and then into Tibetan Buddhism which you can see today in tourist-specific ceremonies in Lhasa, the capital of Tibet and other tour stops.

We will look at the misuse of the word "shaman." A shaman is not an African Witch Doctor nor a North American Medicine man.

A shaman can be male or female, young or old. This will be considered as well as the tools of the trade are all described along with the role of trance, possession and Altered States of Consciousness [ASC].

The book is complimentary to my books on Reiki. There is a direct link between the Shaman's Helping Spirits and the Reiki Guides that helps Reiki practitioners bring healing and comfort to people worldwide during Reiki sessions.

This book is part of a series which includes broad introductions into shamans and shamanism. This book concentrates on reincarnation and the beliefs and rituals that surround the soul. This book is connected to an episode of The Shaman Podcast.

The Reiki, Shamanism and the essential loving mysticism is complementary to our:
- YouTube video series, "Reiki and Shamanism,"
- "The Shaman Podcast" on iTunes, Spotify, Google Podcasts, iHeart Radio, Stitcher, Tunine, Deezer and more.

Connect with our Private Facebook group to learn more about Reiki. Click here.
Subscribe to our newsletter to learn more about Reiki and Shamanism. Click here

Enjoy.
Mark Ashford, MSc,
https://www.markaashford.com

The Shaman

Text Copyright 2016 Mark A. Ashford Consulting Inc.
All Rights Reserved
ISBN: 978-1-988441-41-2

2 Table of Contents

1	Introduction	1
2	Table of Contents	3
3	Table of Figures	5
4	Tibet	9
5	How Long have Shamans and Shamanism Existed?	13
6	History	14
7	Who is a Shaman?	20
7.1	*The etymology of the word Shaman*	*23*
7.2	*differences between Shaman and Mediums.*	*27*
7.3	*Shamans in Nepal*	*27*
8	White, Black and Yellow Shamans	30
8.1	*Mongolia*	*30*
9	Role of the Shaman	33
9.1	*Healer and Guide*	*33*
9.2	*Oracle*	*34*
9.3	*Continuity*	*36*
9.4	*Protector*	*36*
10	Bon Religion	39
10.1	*Primary Differences Between Buddhism and Bon*	*41*
10.2	*Shamanism and Animism*	*42*
10.3	*Bon Sarma*	*43*
10.4	*Mixed Bon*	*43*
10.5	*Bo Murgel*	*43*
10.6	*Dzogchen?*	*43*
11	Five Spiritual Elements in Tibetan Shamanism	45
11.1	*Earth*	*45*
11.2	*Water*	*46*

11.3	Fire	47
11.4	Air	47
11.5	Space	48
11.6	Imbalance of Elements	48
11.7	Cause	51

12 Shaman V's a Medicine Man? 53

13 Shaman V's a Witch Doctor? 59

14 Shamanism: Rituals and Spirituality 63

14.1	Drums and drumstick	65
14.2	Songs	66
14.3	Dance	67
14.4	Costumes	68
14.5	Head Band and Head Dress	68
14.6	Cloak	71
14.7	Foot Wear	71
14.8	Alters and Shrines	71
14.9	Modem Korea and Shamanism	75

15 Shamanism: Changing Perceptions 78

16 Sacred Places in Tibet 83

16.1	Mount Kailash	83
16.2	Bon	83
16.3	Hindus	84
16.4	Jains	84
16.5	Potala Palace:	87
16.6	Jokhang Temple	89
16.7	Norbulingka:	92
16.8	Drepung Monastery	94

17 Bibliography: 96

3   Table of Figures

Figure 1. Healing hands of a Shaman 6
Figure 2. Tibet, part of China in lower left, next to India and Nepal 8
Figure 3. Wall Paintings of a Shaman 12
Figure 4. Contemplating Messages from a Journey 32
Figure 5. Divining the path forward 38
Figure 6. Tibetan Prayer Flags in the colours of the five elements with Mt. Everest 44
Figure 7. Stupas painted in colours of three of the five elements 50
Figure 8. North American Medicine Wheel 52
Figure 9. Closeup of a witch from an indigenous African tribe 58
Figure 10. Tibetan Shaman in full Costume, Drumming and Dancing 62
Figure 11. Drumming 65
Figure 12. A Shaman 70
Figure 13. S. Korean Mudang, Shaman. Ecstasy in Dance 74
Figure 14. Shaman Messages on the wind 77
Figure 15. Sacred Mount Kailash 82
Figure 16. Tibetan Buddhist Monestary 86
Figure 17. Potala Palace 88
Figure 18. Jokhang Temple 89
Figure 19. Buddhist Temple 93

Figure 1. Healing hands of a Shaman

The Shaman

Figure 2. Tibet, part of China in lower left, next to India and Nepal

4   Tibet

Home to Mount Everest and the Himalayas, Tibet, or the "Roof of the World," is the most elevated ecosystem on the planet with altitudes averaging 4,000 metres (2.5 mi.). Landlocked by mountain ranges on its northern, western, and southern borders, Tibet can be divided into three geographical regions:

1. The inhospitable Northern Plateau with its low temperatures, barren climate, and sparse vegetation;

2. The Outer Plateau that most Tibetans call home; Subtropical Southeastern Plateau where the Yangzi, Mekong, and Indus rivers all originate.[1]

Tibet's borders are with Burma, India, Bhutan, Nepal, and China. It has been an isolated country throughout much of its history, and thus little concrete evidence exists regarding its history before the sixth century.

As Tibetans are genetically quite diverse, the exact origins of the Tibetan people pose a greater mystery. Some modern anthropologists trace the origins of the Tibetan people to the Mongoloid race, characterized by round skulls and short statures. Others believe that the Tibetan ancestors were of Indo-European descent, characterized by a long skull and limbs. But whatever the genetic origins of the Tibetan people, two common myths or traditions of origin exist among the Tibetan people themselves.[2]

1. Based on a letter written by an Indian holy man, an Indian king named Rupati fled to Tibet after suffering defeat in an epic war against the Pandavas. King Rupati's followers sought refuge with him, and their migration and settlement resulted in modern-day Tibetans.

2. The Buddhist deity of compassion Chenresig took the form of a monkey and fathered six children with a mountain giantess in modern day Gangpo. The offspring developed into human ancestors of the Tibetan people.

Tibet's documented history begins with the remarkable reign of Songtsen Gampo from 630 to 649.[3]

---

[1] Diana Lin, "A Brief History of Tibet Autonomous Region," *Harvard University Graduate School of Education*.
[2] Ibid.
[3] Ibid.

A young highly energetic and motivated ruler he made Tibet into an influential force and he helped to mould Tibetan identity. As Tibet expanded its sphere of influence, it created pressure on China's border and instead of going to war, they offered two princesses in marriage.

Both new wives were devout Buddhists. As a result, Songtsen Gampo commissioned temples and monasteries, but he used money from his wives' dowries to send ministers to India to devise writing for the Tibetan people. The resulting Tibetan script in use today is thus a changed form of the Sanskrit used in Kashmir.

Known as one of the greatest kings of Tibet's history, Songtsen Gampo expanded Tibet's influence and introduced a written language, and popularized Tibetan Buddhism.

Tibet's proximity to China has meant that much of Tibetan history has been written by the Chinese. The Chinese have a much longer history of written language, and it wasn't until the seventh century that the Tibetans adopted a writing system of their own. This script seems to have been created for translating the Buddhist canons brought from India. The recording of Tibetan history was definitely not a top priority, mirroring the example of India, which also has scarce historical records from the time.[4]

The first king of Tibet appeared 2,000 years ago, 418 years after the death of the Buddha Shakyamuni (Prince Gautama Siddharta) and the king's arrival is marked as the beginning of the Tibetan calendar.

The 32nd king, Namri Songsten, expanded the influence of Tibet, making expeditions as far afield as Persia, but it was his successor, Songsten Gampo (c.618-649), who actively spread the teachings of Buddhism throughout the areas under his control. [5]

By the 13th century, Tibet had exploded its influence, as far away as Persia, and won a war with China. By this time, the Mongol armies of Chinggis Khan, who had already subjugated China, were preparing to attack Tibet.

The Mongol Army, which had already reached eastern Europe, attacked Tibet and in the face of this aggression, the country accepted them as rulers. Tibetan Buddhism and its teachings impressed the Mongol emperors. So much so, the accepted Tibetan Buddhism within the Mongol Empire. The result was that the Mongols became zealous advocates, and the head lama of the powerful Sakyapa [Buddhist] order in Tibet was appointed as head religious figure in the empire, enabling the order to take control of Tibet.

---

[4] Kotan Publishing, "Mapping the Tibetan World."
[5] Ibid.

Later, the Gelukpa Buddhist order, founded by Tsongkhapa (1357–1419), became the dominant school of Tibetan Buddhism in the 16th century. In the 16th century, its leader Sonam Gyatso (1543-88) received the title of "Dalai Lama" from the Mongolian leader Altan Khan. Since then, the Dalai La—mas, who is revered as the incarnation of Avalokiteshvara, has wielded both political and religious power over the country. [6]

By the 19th century, Tibet was in a state of self-imposed isolation. This is when the Asian countries around it were changing dramatically, especially India, which was under British Colonial rule. Up to this point, there had always been a close relationship between Tibet and China, both through religion and intermarriage of royal families.

However, Indian and British Colonial forces invaded in 1903-4 to both take control of Tibet and prevent Russian expansion in the region. A peace and trade treaty signed with an independent Tibetan administration. This provoked the Chinese to intervene and arrange for a separate treaty to be signed with themselves in 1907. A demonstration that Tibet was no longer a separate sovereign country able to complete its own treaties.

By 1910, the Chinese attacked and seized control of Tibet, causing the 13th Dali Lama to flee. Shortly after, nationalist forces seized China and declared a republic. Chinese forces were driven out of Tibet and the 13th Dali Lama returned and declared Tibet a republic.

The freedom last only until 1950 when Chinese Communist troops, Tibet and seized the capital of eastern Tibet, Chamdo. The 15-year-old, 14th Dalai Lama, had virtually no armed forces and was powerless to resist.

The Tibetan government signed the Peaceful Liberation of Tibet in Beijing a year later.

At the signing of the treaty, a fake official seal was used to legitimize the document. Neither India, Britain nor the United Nations came to the aid of Tibet. Subdivision of Tibet into Chinese prefectures, and regions for administrative purposes removed any Tibetan control, and the population was labelled as "Minority People." The Chinese Cultural Revolution of 1966 onwards saw many of the monasteries, temples and religious shrines damaged further or destroyed. Religious texts and artifacts were removed or stolen.

Today, the influx of Chinese into cities such as the Capital Lhasa, had made the native Tibetan a minority culture. [7]

_____

[6] Ibid.
[7] Ibid.

The Shaman

Figure 3. Wall Paintings of a Shaman

5 How Long have Shamans and Shamanism Existed?

To understand Shamans and Shamanism, we need a vision of history that spans many millennia and includes Shamans, Shamanic Traditions, Yoga and Yogic Traditions, Tibetan Buddhism, and an ancient language, Sanskrit. Our vision will be a broad brush taking in a swath of cultures that mixed and merged across India, and all central and eastern Asia, and north into Siberia!

Better yet, think of a diamond and all its facets. We can look at each facet individually. Each is spectacular and intricate, but it is still a diamond, one diamond, and we appreciate the whole.

6   History

Historically, Shamans appear in European cave paintings dating back to the Paleolithic era. The Paleolithic, or Paleolithic, also known as the Stone Age, is a period of human prehistory and includes the earliest stone tool making and represents 95% of human technological prehistory. On the yardstick of existence, the Paleolithic era started 3.3 million years ago and ended as recently as 11,700 years ago. [8]

The Paleolithic era comprised glacial and interglacial periods, in which the climate periodically fluctuated between warm and cool temperatures. Those walking the earth could not be called humans. The correct term for them is Hominin. They were a diverse group that included some modern humans, humans that resemble us today, but other extinct human species and all immediate ancestors, including members of the genuses Homo, Australopithecus, Paranthropus and Ardipithecus also existed. They lived in small family groups, larger bands or tribes and lived a nomadic, hunter gather, subsistence lifestyle. Population density was very low, as low as one person per square mile.

As the Stone Age name implies, stone tools were an important development, but wood and bone tools were also used. Clothing would have been the skins of animals they killed or scavenged. Farming had not appeared.

When vegetation, hunting, and fishing became poor and did not support their group, they moved until they found a new location that provided for their needs. The land gave, and they received. When it did not give, and if they did not move, they died.

By the end of the Paleolithic, several factors coalesced, social organization became more complex, and humans started to produce works of art, cave paintings appeared along with rock art and jewellery. Notably, they started to engage in religious behaviour, such as burial rituals, and rituals connected with successful hunting. It was that humans first began to believe in a pantheon of gods or supernatural beings. They were trying to understand the relationship between the world they saw around them, and over which they had little influence, and the unseen world that helped them explain events and outcomes.

Imagine for a moment a group of hunters preparing to leave to hunt for food but first carrying out rituals asking the spirit of the animals they intend to hunt to allow them to be successful. The Spirits they were praying to are asked to provide animals for them to kill, toned and clothe themselves. If the hunt is fruitful, those rituals will be repeated the next time they hunt. Successful hunting is a confirmation of the ritual and reinforces it. The rituals may be embellished to guarantee success next time or increase the bounty on the hunt. When hunting

---

[8] Wikipedia, "Paleolithic."

is unsuccessful, either the rituals were performed poorly, or the Spirits were unhappy and withheld the animals.

Cave paintings are both art and a way of recording events. Anthropologists have suggested that the half man—half animal being in cave paintings found in Australia and western Europe is evidence of early shamanistic practices and ceremonies as they are very like modern practices. Evidence of skin-covered wood frame drums has been found that are strikingly like contemporary drums used by shamans in hunter-gatherer societies today.

At the beginning it was likely that all members of a band or tribe took part in religious ceremonies, but as the pantheon of gods and Spirits grew, along with the intricacies of rituals and observance, interpretation of messages received from the spirit world became more complex. This required a dedicated individual to assume the responsibility of being the intermediary between the tribe, their gods and Spirits, and the Gods and Spirits of the living world around them.

As the role developed, the practitioner would have experimented with altered states of consciousness so they could interact with what they believed to be the spirit world more easily, more intensely and to allow them channel inspiring energy into this world to get a desirable outcome for whatever question they were being asked to answer.

The earliest known undisputed burial of a shaman and, by extension, the earliest undisputed evidence of shamans and shamanic practices dates to the early Upper Paleolithic or about 30,000 years ago in what is now the Czech Republic. [9]

As recently as 2008, a shaman's grave was unearthed in Israel. The grave was constructed and specifically arranged for a petite, elderly, and disabled woman, who was accompanied by exceptional grave offerings. The grave goods comprised 50 complete tortoise shells and select body parts of a wild boar, an eagle, a cow, a leopard, and two martens, as well as a complete human foot. The internment rituals and the method used to construct and seal the grave suggests that this is the burial of a shaman, one of the earliest known from the archaeological record. Several attributes of this burial later become central in the spiritual arena of human cultures worldwide. [10]

In the historical record, shamanism is the oldest widely practised religion across Asia which was once a single cultural area extending over Russia, China, India, Mongolia, Tibet, Nepal and

---

[9] Ibid.
[10] Natalie D. Munro Leore Grosman, and Anna Belfer-Cohen, "A 12,000-Year-Old Shaman Burial from the Southern Levant (Israel)."

Persia; where shamanism was concerned, these were a unified culture.[11] Shamanism predates organized religion we know today by many thousands of years.

From this original shamanism comes Siberian shamanism which was suppressed by the Soviets, but is now making a comeback in the Buryat Republic, the Bon religion, and probably Chinese ancestor-worship. Buddhism spread throughout central Asia after 600 B.C.; Tibet converted from Bon to Buddhism about 800AD; Tibetan Buddhism—usually called Lamastic Buddhism—embraced most of the elements of Bon and Indian Tantrism … becoming a shamanistic religion. Tibetan lamas fall into trances, predict the future, and in many important ways behave exactly like shamans. After 1,300 AD the Mongols converted from shamanism to Lamastic Buddhism, and this faith spread all the way up into Siberia.[12]

There are important elements to this Asian shamanism which do not appear in accounts from north and South America. Although Asian shamans are no slouches for falling into trances, flying away on "spirit journeys" and so forth, there are elements to their religion which are much more concrete than this, less sensational and far more fascinating.[13]

Shamans were traditional tribal healers, anthropologists coined the term and use it to refer to the spiritual and ceremonial leaders among indigenous cultures worldwide. Shamanism[14, 15] is used to describe ancient spiritual practices in indigenous cultures, it is a spiritual and psychotherapeutic healing technique. It is a worldwide religious phenomenon, considered by many anthropologists to be the most ancient and fundamental form of spiritual practice in human life. Although Shamanism is not present today in all societies, it can be found in many at all levels of complexity and sophistication across the world.[16]

Some anthropologists maintain Shaman is the basis of most magician/sorcerer archetypes in folklore.

In modern times the word is overused, and seems to have become, in the minds of the modern illiterate, purely connected with various character classes in computer Role-Playing Games…

---

[11] Chinese Buddhist Encyclopedia, "Shamanism in Mongolia and Tibet."
[12] Ibid.
[13] Ibid.
[14] "Tibet," *Wikipedia*, September 10, 2018, https://en.wikipedia.org/w/index.php?title=Tibet&oldid=858880580.
[15] "Ancient Tibetan Bonpo Shamanism," accessed September 11, 2018, http://www.vajranatha.com/articles/traditions/bonpo.html?showall=1.
[16] "Korean Shamanism," Korean Shamanism, accessed September 12, 2018, http://shamanism.sgarrigues.net/.

The Shaman

The word "Shaman" is believed to come from the Tungus word "saman" which roughly means holder of knowledge. The Tungus group of languages[17] are spoken by people in Eastern Siberia and Manchuria. The word was not known in the west until Russian soldiers occupied the Shamanistic Khanate of Kazanarea[18] in 1552.

Anthropologists started using the term "Shamanism" to describe unconnected magico-religious practices found in many ethnic religions of the world. In North America, indigenous culture Shaman is not used, Medicine Man/Woman is the more correct term. The term Medicine People are also used when gender is not specific.

Elsewhere, the similarity between practice allows us to use Shaman generically. A view of shamanism is that it is a universal spiritual wisdom inherent to all indigenous tribes. As all ancient spiritual practices are rooted in nature, shamanism is the method by which we, as human beings, can strengthen our connection to the natural world.

In the west, for the past 100 years, the terms "Shaman" and "shamanism" have become over used especially in "new-age" culture.

For many in the very heart of a modern, first world, country such as South Korea, Shaman and Shamanism are very real, and very much needed. Modern Korean Shamanism[19] is extremely important to the daily lives of many Koreans here in 2018.[20]

The differentiator between the Shaman in the Third World from the Shaman in the first, is the degree to which the latter has perfected and elaborated the ritual and symbolism accompanying the form, beliefs, and practice of Shamanism. More recently, in the last century or so, there has been a tendency to simplify and accommodate the needs of the modern believer who has shorter attention spans.

Ancient Tibetan shamanism and animism, the pre-Buddhist spiritual and religious culture of Tibet, was known as Bon, a practitioner of these shamanic techniques of ecstasy and ritual magic, the method of working with energy was known as a Bonpo.

---

[17] "Tungusic Languages," *Wikipedia*, September 12, 2018, https://en.wikipedia.org/w/index.php?title=Tungusic_languages&oldid=859276750.
[18] "Khanate of Kazan," *Wikipedia*, August 22, 2018, https://en.wikipedia.org/w/index.php?title=Khanate_of_Kazan&oldid=856050147.
[19] "Korean Shamanism."
[20] "Korean Shamanism Finds New Life in Modern Era | Reuters," accessed September 12, 2018, https://www.reuters.com/article/uk-korea-shamans/korean-shamanism-finds-new-life-in-modern-era-idUSLNE85S00M20120629.

©Mark A. Ashford Consulting Inc.

The Shaman

Bonpo is still the designation for a Shaman in many tribal regions of the Himalayas. But increasingly, over the centuries, the ecstatic Shaman has been replaced by the priestly Lama or ritual expert, and so later Bonpos in Central Tibet also came to fill a role more ritualistic than ecstatic. There is a parallel here to what occurred in ancient India where the rishis or ecstatic of the early Vedic period, who communed directly with the celestial gods during ecstatic flights into the heavens, were later replaced by Brahman priests, experts in performing of rituals and sacrifices to invoke the powers of the gods and ensure their cooperation for human benefit and prosperity.[21]

But this term Bonpo in ancient times appeared to cover several practitioners whether Shaman, magician, or priest. Here there seems to be a strong parallel of the role of the Bonpo in ancient Tibet with that of the Druid in ancient pre-Christian Europe.

Just as the Druidic order was divided into the three functions of the bards, the Vates, and the Druids, who were singers, soothsayers, and magicians respectively, so the ancient pre-Buddhist kingdom of Tibet was said to be protected by the Drung (sgrung) who were bards and singers of epics, the Deu (lde'u) who were soothsayers and diviners, and the Bonpo (Bon-po) who were priests and magicians. Another archaic term closely related to Bonpo was Shen or Shenpo (gshen-po), and this term may have originally designated the Shaman practitioner. The Shen system of practice was transmitted through family lineages, especially in Western and Northern Tibet, then known as the country of Zhang-zhung, so that Shen also came to designate an ancient clan or tribe.[22]

Buddhism, with its monastic system was finally established as the official religion of Tibet in the eleventh century. Prior to this event, the Shen system of practice was transmitted through family lineages, especially in Western and Northern Tibet, then known as the country of Zhang-zhung, so that Shen also came to designate an ancient clan or tribe.

With the establishment of Buddhism as the official religion there was a methodical and conscious amalgamation of the Bon of Zhang-zhung with the Buddhism of Indian origin, especially as this spiritual tradition was represented by the Nyingmapa school in Tibet. Many ancient rituals and practices have been accepted into the Buddhist schools of Indian origin in Tibet.

Tibetan Buddhism is also known as Vajrayana and Tantra and these terms can be used interchangeably. It can be thought of as a mixture of Buddhism and shamanism, with the latter inherited partially from the shamanistic roots of Hinduism that were passed on into Buddhism, as explained above, and the native shamanism of Tibet, best represented by the Bon tradition.

---

[21] "Ancient Tibetan Bonpo Shamanism."
[22] "Ancient Tibetan Bonpo Shamanism."

The Shaman

This rather remarkable combination created many of the unique features of Vajrayana and dream yoga.[23]

Shamanism has another wholly different dynamic and one that is seen across the world. It has an extraterrestrial origin. The principal purpose of the Shaman over the millennia was more than healing and guiding the soul of a dead person in their afterlife before they reincarnate, most important their purpose was to sustain communication between humanity on the earth and Spirits, angels and guides in heaven above.

In this way, the Shaman helped bring humanity out of a crude animal-like existence and made humanity aware of their consciousness. That Shaman is depicted on cave paintings during the Paleolithic period when humans were learning and making their first tools. I don't think, is a coincidence.

The Shaman was the first human to bridge the gap between gods, ancestors on heavenly plains and in the depths of darkness. The Shaman gained knowledge and provided tribes with someone they could turn to for healing and repair. But above all, the Shaman was someone they could turn to for answers when nothing else helped.

The Shaman's religion is one of nature where the human being is a part of nature and not as something existing outside of or in opposition to it.

Living in harmony with the natural environment on a very personal level was natural and unquestioned. The environment was something to be treasured, and respected, not used or abused.

Harmony means balance. The Shaman, through ritual magic and clairvoyant knowledge, could ensure success in the hunt for the tribe by negotiating a covenant between the tribe and the Spirits of the hunted species. The tribe would weather a hard season and survive while no species of animal was hunted in excess or extinction.

---

[23] "Tibetan Dream Yoga – Integraldeeplistening," accessed September 14, 2018, https://www.integraldeeplistening.com/tibetan-dream-yoga/.

7   Who is a Shaman?

The definition of Shaman in the Urban Dictionary is

… One who can interact and mediate with the spirit world on behalf of their community, usually by ecstatic trance techniques (that is their spirit/soul leaves their physical body to travel to a world of pure spirit rather than physical matter) for divination, foretelling the future, information gathering, healing and to receive wisdom. [24]

In shamanistic belief, the world is filled by Spirits that affect all living beings. In our present context, it is important to underline the change of consciousness that the shamanic adopt undergoes and that the fully developed shaman experiences each time he performs a shamanic session. This includes, with Eliade and others—mostly following its "typical" Siberian form—the following aspects.

Spirits exist and play important roles both in individual lives and in human society; they can be good or evil. The shaman can communicate with the spirit world. The male or female adept, after a sudden crisis, believes that he is chosen, is then recreated and educated by the Spirits. He becomes an "embodiment" of his spirit guardian or helping spirit ("familiar") or of his double, an (external) soul in animal form. He then can travel to the other worlds to communicate with the gods and Spirits, in a state of ecstasy exhibited in his rituals.

The shaman employs trance-inducing techniques to incite visionary ecstasy and to go on vision quests. This is achieved by music (drumming), dancing, recitation of certain texts, mantras, etc. The shaman's spirit can leave the body to enter the supernatural world to search for answers. He evokes animal images as spirit guides, omens, and message bearers. He can treat sickness caused by evil Spirits. The shaman can tell the future by crystal gazing, throwing bones or runes; he can also perform many other forms of divination.

Spirits who can influence man's life

- There are general and reciprocal interconnections in nature (humans included);
- Human beings are not superior but are equal to the other forms of life;
- Human society is closely connected with the cosmos;
- It is possible for human beings to gain some qualities of a spirit and visit the other worlds;

---

[24] Urban Dictionary, "Shaman."

The Shaman

- The aim of religious activity is to defend and make prosperous a small group of kin. Or, in more detail, the shamans can be described as:

The ideological background is that humans and Spirits or deities are closely related and interact, especially through the shaman, who ensure the success of the clan in hunting and other activities.

The shaman is usually "called" by spirit or spiritual powers who force him or her to become a shaman, sometimes in their dreams.24 Other shamans choose their career.

The shaman provides a link with several, usually 9, levels of the world, of which we can see only one, our own world. The other ones are those of the Spirits or powers. Shamans move up to them by the axis mundi, symbolized by a tree or a pathway, and bring back knowledge. Or they do so with various (local) animal familiars.

As a healer, the shaman moves to other levels of the universe to find out what the Spirits want, so that sickness and other evils can be overcome. Disease originates with certain Spirits or through witchcraft by evil shamans.

Shamans heal by going to the spirit world, when in trance, and by leaving their own body or transforming into another being, the "familiar." They have one or more "familiar": a particular animal, a double soul, Spirits of healing plants or sometimes those of deceased shamans. Healing proceeds by retrieving the soul of the ill person. Shamans often enter the patient to fight the disease-causing spirit; they heal by driving the spirit out, sometimes by showing an extracted token of the spirit. They also guide the souls of the dead.

Shamans usually are very knowledgeable about local healing plants, learned directly from the Spirits. Rocks or quartz are commonly used because of their special powers and their animating Spirits. They often are spiritually introduced into a shaman.

Shamans help the hunt with magic by releasing the souls of the animals, ensuring that they are not angered or hurt, or by letting a killed animal tell others to be killed.

Shamans may be exposed to risk that originates from the Spirits then engage with, from enemy or malevolent shamans, from some plants they used, from altering their state of consciousness, and by not returning from a spiritual journey, which leads to death. These dangers are lessened by spells.

Returning to consciousness, this world and their body, the shaman transmits the messages of the Spirits or deities. In sum, the shaman is an ancient form of the typical "intermediary." Late this role would become the domain of priests, but he is one who has got and "tamed" special powers that he exercises in trance, including heat.

Clearly, certain psychological features, a change of consciousness and trance are involved in being a shaman. However, the shaman's state of mind is not one of "possession," in the common use of the term, though "possession" and "shamanic trance" are frequently confused.

It is important to distinguish both: on the one hand, the commonly found involuntary phenomenon of possession by a spirit and, on the other, the self-induced shamanic trance that occurs after (initial) contact with the Spirits, showed by shaking. After this initial involuntary or accidental contact with the spirit world, it is the shaman's quest to contact Spirits and the other worlds. While in possession, a spirit enters an unwilling being.

Both possession and trance, however, share one major feature, which has led to the common confusion between the two terms. The initiatory crisis of the future shaman is usually shown by involuntary shaking, induced by the Spirits in some form or other. This state is also called the "shamanic illness." The shamanistic initiatory crisis functions as an—involuntary—rite of passage for the future shaman, and it involves both a more-or-less serious physical illness and/or a psychological crisis. This state is well attested across all shamanic regions. Next to illness, the shaman-to-be may be struck by lightning and may dream of thunder, or may have a near-death experience.

While in this state, Siberian shamans may behave, according to our modern standards, in a psychotic fashion. Local Siberians, on the contrary, interpret this as initiatory "possession" by a spirit who demands that the selected person become a shaman. However, the shaman does not remain "possessed" after the initial crisis, but undergoes a long period of training by other shamans. He can then freely call on his spirit (the familiar), when he wishes to go into a trance. All of this is quite unlike the involuntary "possession" by some kind of demon or spirit. In some societies, shamans gain a personality split into two Spirits; this includes shamanic dress and attributes, the role or function of the other sex or gender fluidity and/or same-sex sexual orientation.

There are several seemingly global characteristics that unit San, Andamanese, Australian and Eurasian/Amerindian shamanism. Some aspects of these characteristics are already clearly, some others likely, represented in Stone-Age rock art: death and rebirth/change inside the body; use of animal familiars; trance: descent/ascent to the Spirits or deities; contact with and use of supermundane powers for healing and success in hunting; management of heat in the spinal cord; shape-shifting/animal costume; dance and music, i.e. "musical spots" in caves; transmitting such knowledge in songs and tales, creating early mythologies.

This congruence seems to reflect an older stage of shamanism. Importantly, several of the key shamanistic features—new body, ascent to the deities as a bird, dance, contact with powers, and connection with hunting magic—are seen already in Cro-Magnon paintings.

These paintings are archaeologically datable, at least, to the later part of the Upper Paleolithic, from c. 27,000—14,000 BCE. Further, some important features, such as shamanistic dance, animal costume or shape-shifting, hunting magic, communication with Spirits and the transmission of tales present in reconstructed Stone-Age mythology Gondwana and Laurasian fit well into early hunter societies' conceptions of shamanic power. They include items such as the shaman's death and rebirth during initiation, the (parallel) rebirth of animals killed in hunting, his ascent to heaven and return to earth.

7.1 The etymology of the word Shaman

The etymology of the word Shaman has changed over the many millennia.

The term "shamanism" was first applied by Western anthropologists as outside observers of the ancient religion of the Turks and Mongols, as well as those of the neighbouring Tungstic- and Samoyedic-speaking peoples. Upon observing more religious traditions across the world, some Western anthropologists began to also use the term in a very broad sense. The term was used to describe unrelated magico-religious practices found within the ethnic religions of other parts of Asia, Africa, Australasia and even completely unrelated parts of the Americas, as they believed these practices to be like one another. [25]

There are four broad definitions describing a shaman though none are widely agreed: [26]

1. Someone who contacts a spirit world while in an altered state of consciousness.

2. Someone who contacts a spirit world while in an altered state of consciousness at the behest of others.

3. The shaman is defined by their techniques or abilities, which separate them from and other magico-religious specialists who are believed to contact Spirits, such as mediums, witch doctors, spiritual healers, and prophets.

    - The first problem with this definition is that researchers cannot agree on the techniques and abilities of the shaman processes the others do not.

---

[25] Wikipedia, "Shamanism."
[26] Ibid.

- The second issue is that the term shaman has become somewhat of a paintbrush for all magico-religious specialists in other parts of Asia, Africa, Australasia and unrelated parts of the Americas, as they believed these practices to be like one another.

4. The shaman is defined within the boundaries of indigenous religions in Siberia and neighbouring parts of Asia.

The shaman is a person, male or female, young, or old, who a shamanic spirit guide has worked with and helps become a shaman who will then perform the role of intermediary between the physical and non-physical realms. There is a unique bond between the physical person and their shamanic spirit guide. They become family.

Other helping Spirits become part of the connection between the physical and spiritual, but there will always be one core connection, rather like the way we have circles of friends and one or a few very close ones.

A phenomenon called "shamanistic initiatory crisis," a rite of passage for shamans-to-be, commonly involving physical illness or psychological crisis. The significant role of initiatory illnesses in the calling of a shaman can be found in the detailed case history of Chuonnasuan, [27] who was the last master shaman among the Tungus peoples in Northeast China. [28]

The wounded healer is an archetype for a shamanic trial and journey. This process is important to young shamans. They undergo a type of sickness that pushes them to the brink of death. This is said to happen for two reasons:

- The shaman crosses over into the underworld. This happens so the shaman can venture to its depths to bring back vital information for the sick and the tribe. The shaman must become sick to understand sickness. When the shaman overcomes their own sickness, they believe they will hold the cure to heal all that suffer.

- Shamans are intermediaries or messengers between the human world and the spirit worlds.

Shamanic activities are typically concerned with health. The shaman's rituals played an essential role in the psychic defence of the community, defending "life, health, fertility, the world of light, against death, diseases, sterility, disaster, and the world of darkness.

---

[27] Kun Shi Richard Noll, "Chuonnasuan. The Last Shaman of the Oroqen of Ne China," *Journal of Korean Religions, 2004.*
[28] Wikipedia, "Shamanism."

The Shaman

Shamans treat ailments and illness by repairing damage to the soul of the person seeking treatment. The theories of illness typically focus on soul loss, which was considered being caused by Spirits' aggression or by theft by other shamans. Other prominent causes of illness were thought to involve spirit aggression and sorcery where health was affected by the actions of ghosts and Spirits, or the malevolent action of other shamans, sorcerers, or witches. Shamanic rituals typically involved the dramatic enactment of struggles with Spirits to remove them and recover the patient's soul. Besides spirit-focused rituals with a variety of socio- and psychotherapeutic functions, the shaman's healing ceremonies also incorporated physical medicine—cleansing of wounds, extraction of objects, and the use of herbal medicine.

The shamanic universe is based on animism, a belief in spirit entities that effects on all aspects of human life. Spirits were the essence of natural forces and humans, as well as the animals on which the shamans depended on their powers. Developing relationships with the Spirits was central to training of shamans, with animal spirit helpers the bases of shamanic powers and the agents through which the shaman carries out a variety of activities. A common belief was that the shaman accomplished tasks in the guise of animals into which the shaman transformed.

Let's step back for a moment. We need to be clear about the world of Spirits and souls.

You, I, and everything living in the world around has a spirit, a soul, a life force. Shamans and many world religions believe in reincarnation.[29] Reincarnation is a philosophical or religious belief that all living things, especially humans, contain a non-physical essence, and that when the body of a living being ends, that non-physical essence begins a new life in a different physical form or body. It may also be called rebirth or transmigration.

The non-physical soul or spirit is here in the physical world to learn, learn from their physical existence, they can do well by helping people, but also by not mistreating others because of a perceived injury from another. In the Buddhist view, the soul is gathering merit.[30]

Merit[31] is a fundamental notion in Buddhist ethics. It is a beneficial and protective force which accumulates because of good deeds, acts, or thoughts. Merit-making is important to Buddhist practice: merit brings good and agreeable results, determines the quality of the next life and contributes to a person's growth towards enlightenment. In addition, merit is also shared with a deceased loved one, to help the deceased in their new existence. Despite modernization, merit-making remains essential in traditional Buddhist countries and has had a significant impact on the rural economies in these countries.[32] The opposite of Merit is Demerit. Demerit

---

[29] "Reincarnation.Pdf."
[30] "Merit Buddhism."
[31] Ibid.
[32] Ibid.

brings retribution and weakens the merit already accumulated. A mixture of the two generates mixed results in a person's life.

In the world of a shamanism, the soul or spirit may not go immediately to the next physical form. They may linger in the current world as a non-physical essence and may attach themselves to a physical person, and if malevolent, the soul may hurt or damage the physical person they have attached to. The soul damage manifests itself as illness, or even causes the physical person to do harm to others.

A Shaman by healing the soul or spirit of a person, restores the physical body of the individual to balance and wholeness. The Shaman encounters the source of the sickness and can guide the spirit to the spirit world, where they can manifest into a new physical being healed and capable of continuing their journey.

Shamans operate primarily within the spiritual world, which, they believe, affects the human world. The restoration of balance is said to result in the ailment's elimination.

Shamans use divination to gather answers to many questions, from questions affecting an individual to an entire tribe. In this way, they were also advisers to leaders or a council of leadership. Genghis Khan, renowned for his military prowess, was primarily a shaman steeped in Tengriism. Mongolian shamanism is centred on the worship of the Tngri (gods) and the highest Tenger (Heaven, God of Heaven, God) or Qormusta Tengri. [33]

Divination gives answers to all the questions in life. Shamanic practitioners use three primary divination techniques: [34]

1. Journeying. In journeying, the practitioner enters the spirit world to access information directly from the source. Basically, shamanic journeying is a way of communicating with your inner or spirit self and retrieving information. Your inner self is in constant communication with all aspects of your environment, seen and unseen. You need only journey within to find answers to your questions. After the journey, you must then interpret the meaning of your trance experience.

2. Spirit embodiment: In the embodiment trance to bring a helping spirit into the practitioner's body. In an embodiment trance, the practitioner asks the spirit helpers to come into ordinary reality, enter the practitioner's body, and impart information through them. The idea is to become like a hollow bone, a conduit for spirit. By becoming an empty vessel for spirit, we can access the invisible sea of information that we bathe in daily, the all-pervading frequencies of

---

[33] Wikipedia, "Mongolian Shamanism."
[34] Michael Drake, "Shamanic Drumming Shamanic Divination."

consciousness in all phenomena. Drumming is an excellent way to induce a divination trance, allowing the practitioner to perceive energetic frequencies in a unique way. The practitioner experiences energies and then interprets them through his or her own symbolic language.

3. Divination tools: When using a divination tool, the practitioner enters an altered state and allows the patterns in the tool to determine the message from the spirit. One of the best-known divination tools is the I Ching. The I Ching is a microcosm of all possible human situations. It serves as a dynamic map; whose function is to reveal one's relative position in the cosmos of events. The hexagram texts address the sixty-four archetypal human situations. The commentary of each hexagram reveals the optimal strategy for integrating or harmonizing with the inevitable for a condition. It appropriately responds to your inquiry. It affords a holistic perspective of your current condition and discusses the proper way to address the situation

7.2   differences between Shaman and Mediums.

The differences between shamans and mediums involve the consequences of the different socioeconomic conditions under which each type of shamanistic healer is found. The shamans were associated with animal Spirits and hunting magic, sickness and health reflecting their subsistence patterns as foragers, while mediums were involved in agricultural rituals. Mediums had lower social and economic status than shamans, while shamans had high social esteem derived from their informal political power and preeminent roles in group leadership. Mediums are predominantly women and of low social status, as opposed to shamans, who are predominantly men and of high social status. Shamans were also involved in malevolent activities designed to magically harm their enemies, an activity absent from mediums.

The differences between shamans and mediums are particularly seen in the medium's Altered State of Consciousness (ASC), which is characterized by the experience of possession where a spirit is thought to take over the person's behaviour. Although both shamans and mediums undergo experiences during the selection period in which they have illness, involuntary dreams, or visions, full mediums are more likely to continue to have experiences that occur beyond their control or intention. Although it was believed that sometimes the shamans' Spirits could be out of their direct control, shamans were thought to control the Spirits. This is in stark contrast to the mediums, who are thought to act under compulsion from the spirit world. Even though the medium intends to enter an ASC, these experiences are thought to involve possession of the medium, who is believed to be controlled by the possessing spirit.

7.3   Shamans in Nepal

The Banjhākri [Ban jhākri][35] and Banjhākrini [Ban Jhākrini] are a couple, the Banjhākri is the male, and the Banjhākrini is his mate. They are shamanic deities in the tradition of the Tamang people of Nepal.

The Banjhākri is a traditional forest deity and god.[36] In the Nepali language, ban means "wilderness," jhākri means "shaman," and Jhākrini means "shamaness." Banjhākrini is also known as Lemlemey.[37] A shaman, a teacher, an initiator of great things. A descendent of the Sun. A trickster and abductor of children and adults. Any abduction, of boys or girls, is not doing so out of malice. Those abducted are believed by the Banjhākri to have the gifts of shamanism in their blood, their bones, their soul.

By tradition, the Banjhākri take the abductee back to their cave and there he taught the student about the forest, spirits, life, death, and healing. Taught in this way, when the abductee was returned to their home, their village, their community, after a few days, they were more powerful than any shaman taught by a human. They are prototypical models for becoming a shaman in Nepal and, so to speak, a mark of distinction and an epithet of supernatural potency and unofficial status. The abductee may be taken again for further training. The Banjhākri may also appear in dreams to continue teaching.

If the abductee were found to have physical problems, scars, or not pure of heart, or if they failed the initiation ceremony at the end of their stay, or had been disobedient, they would be thrown out of the Banjhakri camp and risked being captured by his ferocious and cannibalistic mate, the Banjhakrini who would kill them with her gold cycle and eat their bodies.

In all the stories about the Banjhakri, they are the teacher, the guide, the instructor, the leader, the mentor, but now he wanted to learn. They teach using a combination of telepathy and a secret language the initiate learns.

Like the yeti, Banjhakri and Banjhakrini can be seen in our world, and not just in the spirit world. However, only powerful shamans can see them. Although both Banjhakri and yeti are apelike, yeti is taller than humans, whereas Banjhakri is only about 1–1.5 m (3–5 feet) tall.[38] Both have fur covering their entire body except for their hands and their face. Their feet face backwards. This means if tracks are found, the trackers are inevitably going in the wrong direction if they follow the impressions believing them to be normal human feet. The yeti lives in the high mountain pass and are teachers of yogi and others that seek the peace and energy of high mountains and live there in caves.

---

[35] Wikipedia, "Banjhakri and Banjhakrini."
[36] Larry G. Peters, "The "Calling," the Yeti, and the Ban Jhakri ("Forest Shaman") in Nepalese Shamanis."
[37] Wikipedia, "Banjhakri and Banjhakrini."
[38] Peters, "The "Calling," the Yeti, and the Ban Jhakri ("Forest Shaman") in Nepalese Shamanis."

The Banjhakri are the masters of liminality. They stand at the juncture of two realities, in between categories and boundaries. They are physical and spiritual. Human and animal, beings of dreams and of reality. They are the masters in a numinous unbounded space where everything is backwards, opposite, and dangerous. They are the neophytes' guides through the dark night before initiatory rebirth. [39]

---

[39] Ibid.

8 White, Black and Yellow Shamans

8.1 Mongolia

Mongol shamanism has ninety-nine deities sacred in symbolic of numerals in the Mongol mentality.[40] Fifty-five deities were White, i.e., Beneficial for humanity. The other forty-four were Black, i.e., Evil, to humanity and to the enemies of the Mongol Nation. All ninety-nine deities were the national gods of Mongol Shamanism. These were the Spirits of Ancestors of every clan, the souls of dead chieftains, shamans and shamanesses who during their life had devoted themselves to satisfying the members of clans and who in the World of Spirits should solve the difficulties in the life of the members of their clans, commoners and nobles and even serfs.[41]

After the White and Black gods, there were the innumerable minor genii—the Spirits of a clan's ancestors, divided into several classes. The largest among them were the class of the souls of the clans' chieftains, introduced after their death by a special solemn shamanist right to the Communion of Clan Ancestors and thus becoming members of the Communion and of the Benevolent Lord-Spirits who played a very important role in the life of a clan and its members. Everybody could appeal to the Lord-Spirits of his clan, worship them, and make offerings to them through the mediation of the shamans and shamanesses. In extraordinary cases, everyone could invite the Great Shaman fi'yarin or the Great Shamaness to make an appeal to the Lord-Spirits and await their invigorating reply or spiritual help, which could increase the moral and material support of the entire clan to its members.

The gods and deities of the Mongols fell into the following hierarchy:[42]

White and Black deities
Lord-Spirits of the clan
Protector-Spirits of the clan
Guardian-Spirits of the clan
White Spirits of Nobles of the clan
Black Spirits of Commoners of the clan
Evil Spirits

White Shaman or Shamaness could worship the Black Spirits but immediately they did so, they became Black Shamans or Shamanesses and had no right of dedication to the Terrifying Black

---

[40] Yönsiyebü Rinchen, "White, Black and Yellow Shamans among the Mongols," *Ultimate Reality and Meaning* 4, no. 2 (1981).
[41] Ibid.
[42] Ibid.

Spirits and simultaneously lost the right to adore and worship the Benevolent White Spirits. The white spirits never victimize a White Shaman and Shamanesses who turns to Black spirits. But terror and retribution from vindictive Black spirits would prevent them from ever again worshipping White Spirits.

After the establishment of the Great Mongol Empire of Chinggis Khan, his Borjigin clan became the Golden (Imperial) clan, towering above all Mongol clans. The Lord-Spirits, the Protector-Spirits, the Guardian-Spirits of the BorJigin clan were raised to the high rank of the Ancestor-Spirits of the whole Nation of Mongols.

The establishment of Buddhism in Mongolia and the adoption of Buddhism by the Borjigin clan resulted in White Shamans and Shamanesses accepting willingly the new Yellow Religion, "Yellow" being the Saffron colour of Buddhist robes. White Shamans and Shamanesses embracing Buddhism received the title "Yellow Shamans and Shamanesses." Black Shamans and Shamanesses did not/do not accept Buddhism.

Many of these Yellow Shamans and Shamanesses had the books of shamanist prayers and hymns in Mongolian transcribed by monks with the Tibetan syllabic characters as Buddhist books of prayers, and the monks and Yellow Shamans believed that a Mongol text transcribed with Tibetan characters is eight times more blessed than the same text written in Mongol letters. [43]

---

[43] Ibid.

Figure 4. Contemplating Messages from a Journey

9 Role of the Shaman

9.1 Healer and Guide

The shaman is a healer. This is their principal role in the tribe, the community.

They have access to, and influence in, the world of benevolent and malevolent spirits, who typically enter a trance state during a ritual, and practices divination and healing.

Soul journeying to understand what and why a person was ill and journeying to spirits that will help return health to the physical person is their primary and most essential role.

Mongol shamanism had ninety-nine deities:

- Fifty-five deities were White, i.e., Beneficent for humanity.
- Forty-four were Black, i.e., Terribles to all the evildoers of humanity and to the enemies of the Mongol Nation.

They are the national gods of Mongol Shamanism. No commoner of any Mongol clan dared embarrass them with his insubstantial bagatelle, since they were the Spirits of Ancestors of every clan, the souls of dead chieftains, shamans and shamanesses who during their life had devoted themselves to satisfying the members of clans and who in the World of Spirits should solve the difficulties in the life of the members of their clans, commoners, and nobles and even serfs. [44]

Minor spirits of a clan's ancestors divided into several classes. The largest among them were the class of the souls of the clans' chieftains, introduced after their death by a special solemn shamanist right to the Communion of Clan Ancestors and thus becoming members of the Communion and of the Benevolent Lord-Spirits who played a very important role in the life of a clan and its members.

Black shamanism is a kind of shamanism practised in Mongolia and Siberia. It is specifically opposed to yellow shamanism, which incorporates rituals and traditions from Buddhism. Black Shamans are usually perceived as working with evil spirits, while white Shamans with spirits of the upper world.

Other Souls and Spirits included…

---

[44] Ibid.

- Souls of the Great Shamans: Protector-Spirits of the Clan
- Souls of the Simple Shamans: Guardian-Spirits of Localities
- The Three Spirits Accepting Supplication

<u>Division of the gods and spirits of Mongol shamanism:</u>

- White and Black deities
- Lord-Spirits of the clan
- Protector-Spirits of the clan
- Guardian-Spirits of the clan
- White Spirits of Nobles of the clan
- Black Spirits of Commoners of the clan
- Evil Spirits

Chinggis Khan, or Genghis Khan, the renowned Mongolian leader practised Black Shamanism though he, himself was not a shaman.

The banner at the head of the Mongol Armies that subjugated China and got as far as eastern Europe was black. But this should not be confused with Chinggis Khan and his practice of Black Shamanism. A tribe would have black and white banners in the centre of their camp.

The banners were each guarded together with white and black Lord Spirits of the Clan. Nobles of the clan would escort the banners during ceremonies and feasts.

In battle, the black banner was believed to bring victory over Mongol enemies while the white banner remained in camp.

9.2 Oracle

Shaman was astrologers and Oracles. Everyone, especially tribal leaders, wants to know what the future will bring. Will it bring war? Will they be successful in the struggle? Will crops and animal husbandry be successful? Will the tribe merge with another through marriage?

The history of the shaman in this role goes back into the very remote past, before Buddhism in Tibet in the seventh century.

Historically, these Oracles, divination and Astrology were a feature of Bon in pre-Buddhist Tibet. The Bon cosmology was divided into three worlds.

1. The upper world of the gods.

2. An intermediate world of spirits, of subtle beings.

3. The solid or physical world we know as the earth.

Bon also held the spirit or soul of the individual, which was a world or realm of energy which humans can contact. For example, humans can connect with physical things such as food, a chair and other people. On the spiritual level, they can connect at the psychic level with other spirits and those on the different levels, such as the first and second.

When Buddhists brought Buddhist Dharma to Tibet, they could include the Bon world view into their own because Buddhism holds the view. The Buddhist world exists in three parts: one solid, one psychic, and one mental.

The change happened when the famous Tantric master Guru Padmasambhava came to Tibet and tamed the subtle world—the deities of the Bonpos—and bound them under oath to obey and defend the Buddhist teaching. He made these powers, which we can call deities, protectors of the Buddhist faith and of Buddhist practitioners. They became Cho sung, protectors of the Dharma. According to Tibetan tradition, he tamed these beings through the powerful invocation of mantras, powerful spells, which bound them to obey those who held the power of these spells. Guru Padmasambhava tamed these beings. He made them protectors of the Dharma and convinced them to help practitioners of Buddha Dharma by communicating, giving advice, foretelling the future and even healing people.[45]

The deities are sentient beings. They are beings, just like people or animals and anyone else, but without a body. They also have a mind or spirit, and a voice. Without a body, they cannot communicate with those who communicate on a bodily level. So, they are samsaric beings.

Samsara is the term for the everlasting cycle of being. It is the cycle of becoming and passing away, or the cycle of rebirths in the Indian religions of Hinduism, Buddhism, and Jainism.

They are not higher gods, as we would understand the great gods of India or Tibet. They are gods linked to the land, mountains, lakes and to the geographical features. We could say that mountains and lakes are their bodily aspect. So, they are the subtle aspect: the speech and mind aspect of mountains, valleys, rivers and lakes, especially mountains and lakes.

---

[45] Dr Fabian Sanders, "Tibetan Oracles and Himalayan Shamans."

9.3 Continuity

They were the spiritual leader of a group or tribe. The belief and practice of Shamanism incorporate a range of beliefs, customs, ceremonies and rituals regarding communication with the spiritual world in which their religious leader, the Shaman, enters supernatural realms particularly when the tribe is facing adversity or need to get solutions to problems afflicting the community including sickness.[46]

They provided continuity to the tribe and a reliable connection to the spirit world. In this way, they were a communicator from the human physical world to the spirit world and back again.

They were an educator of people about the spirit world and about medicines and herbs and natural healing solutions. They kept the tribal stories, myths and essential tribal wisdom that made the tribe they belonged to different from another.

They understood and passed down understanding of trance states, how to induce them and how to control them. Their clothing, symbolic regalia and objects were passed down to enrich subsequent generations of shaman.

They are the keepers of tradition, ancient texts, books, and scripts and the way things should be done. Songs, dances, music, and observance are also carried forward from the shaman to shamans within the tribe.

Shamans usually have expert knowledge of medicinal plants native to their area, and an herbal treatment is often prescribed. It is believed shamans learn directly from the plants, harnessing their effects and healing properties, after obtaining permission from the indwelling or patron spirits.[47]

The chieftains and nobles may change, but the shaman remains.

9.4 Protector

One of a shaman's major functions is to protect individuals from hostile supernatural influences.

The shaman may act as a psychopomp, conducting the spirits of individuals who have just died to the proper refuge for dead spirits.

---

[46] warpaths2peacepipes.com, "Shaman."
[47] Wikipedia, "Shamanism."

Psychopomp literally means "guide of souls" are creatures, spirits, angels, or deities in many religions whose responsibility is to escort newly deceased souls from Earth to the afterlife. They do not judge the deceased, but simply to guide them. Appearing frequently on funerary art, psychopomps have been depicted at different times and in different cultures as anthropomorphic entities, horses, deer, dogs, whip-poor-wills, ravens, crows, vultures, owls, sparrows and cuckoos. When seen as birds, they are often seen in vast masses, waiting outside the home of the dying.[48]

---

[48] "Psychopomp."

Figure 5. Divining the path forward

10 Bon Religion

Bon is an ancient shamanist religion. It is indigenous to the Himalayas and Central Asia. Especially the Tibetan region, the religion contains rituals, exorcisms, talismans, spells, incantations, drumming, sacrifices, a pantheon, god, good and evil spirits, and a cult of the dead or ancestor worship.

While there is almost no written tradition of the early pre-Buddhist indigenous religious practices in the region, Bon has a coherent and unified system of doctrines based on a vast literature, over 1,000 years old.[49]

It is the main aboriginal religion of the ancient Qinghai-Tibetan Plateau. It is said to have originated in the 5th century B.C. with Shenrab Miwoche, the prince of the Zhang-zhung kingdom in western Tibet. This means it predates Buddhism, which arrived in the seventh century AD by a long way.

Around the first century A.D., the religion began to spread eastward until it became widely practised in the Tsang and Lhasa regions. Bon is still practised today. It embraces pantheism and believes that "everything has a soul." Bon deities include supernatural powers of mountains, rivers, lakes, seas, the sun, the moon, stars, wind, rain, thunder, lightning, birds, and beasts, one can enumerate. These deities govern the birth, ageing, sickness, death, events and fortunes of people, who cannot predict and control their own destinies because people have been created by the deities.[50]

Yungdrung Bon is the teaching of the Central Asian Buddha, Tonpa Shenrab Miwoche, who lived and preached in the heart of Tagzig, an ancient country located somewhere in the Pamir Mountains, possibly in modern-day Tajikistan and/or the surrounding Central Asian republics. The teachings of this Buddha were brought into and flourished in the land of Zhang Zhung, an empire or tribal confederations centred in western Tibet around Tise (Mount Kailash). It is from this heartland that Yungdrung Bon reached Tibet, initially a small vassal state of Zhang Zhung which eventually overthrew its overlord in the sixth-eighth centuries AD. Yungdrung Bon is divided into two major parts, Causal and Fruitional. In a nutshell, Bon comprises a vast body of rituals designed to improve worldly conditions and lessen hardships in this life and gradually guide the practitioner towards the higher teachings of Fruitional Bon, which ultimately lead to Buddhahood.[51]

---

[49] Rubin Museum of Art, "Bon Press Release."
[50] CATHOLICS AND SUPERSTITION IN TIBET BON RELIGION, "Bon Religion, Catholics and Superstition in Tibet."
[51] Dmitry Ermakov, "Bo and Bon - Ancient Shamanic Traditions of Siberia and Tibet in Their Relation to the Teachings of a Central Asian Buddha."

When Tonpa Shenrab came to Tibet, which, according to the well-known 20th-century Buddhist scholar Gedun Chophel, he blessed Tibet and its people, sharing many teachings, ceremonies and religious dances that are distinctly Bon. The most important change he introduced was to eliminate animal sacrifice.

The local practice was to sacrifice animals in order to appease spirits responsible for causing sickness and misfortune. Tonpa Shenrab taught them they could offer red torma and white torma in place of animals. Torma are figures made mostly of flour and butter used in tantric rituals or as offerings in Tibetan Buddhism. They may be dyed in different colours, often white or red for the main body. They are made in specific shapes based on their purpose, usually conical in form.[52] In this way, Tonpa Shenrab established the peaceful, enlightened Yungdrung-Bon tradition. [53]

Bon is rooted in nature, recognizing its aliveness and spiritual dimension. Bonpos, as the practitioners are called, cultivate strong relationships with the spiritual dimension through rituals, symbolic offerings and prayers. They believe that there are many kinds of beings that can affect one in both positive and negative ways. By maintaining awareness of such possibilities, one can work with the various spirits to eliminate obstacles as well as receive help.[54]

Many Bonpo practices and meditations are unique, most especially the Bon Five Element practice.

In the Bon tradition, the universe comprises five elements. In fact, our body is composed of five elements (earth, water, fire, wind and space). These five are expressed within us through the interconnection of flesh, blood, heat, breath, and consciousness. They are connected to the five organs: liver, kidneys, spleen, lungs and heart. Those organs are connected to the five poisons; attachment, jealousy, ignorance, pride, and anger. The five poisons can be transformed into the five wisdoms: emptiness, mirror-like wisdom, wisdom of equality, discriminating wisdom, and all-accomplishing wisdom. The transformation of the five poisons into the five wisdoms is the basis of spiritual practice. Each element has its own corresponding spiritual deity. All sentient beings are connected with their inner, their outer [environmental], as well as the natural form of each element. In this way, Bon developed distinctly.[55]

---

[52] Wikipedia, "Torma."
[53] buddhaweekly.com/, "Iinterview-Bon-Teacher-Chaphur-Rinpoche-Explains-Bon-Different-Similar-Five-Buddhist-Schools-Tibet."
[54] Bon: Indigenous Shamanism of Tibet, "Bon- Indigenous Shamanism of Tibet."
[55] buddhaweekly.com/, "Iinterview-Bon-Teacher-Chaphur-Rinpoche-Explains-Bon-Different-Similar-Five-Buddhist-Schools-Tibet."

The Shaman

Prayer flags, prayers wheels, sky burials, festival devil dances, spirit traps, rubbing holy stones—things that are associated with Tibetan religion and Tibetan Buddhism—all developed from Bon.[56]

When Buddhism became established in Tibet, Bonpos recognized many Buddhist traditions were wise and effective and began incorporating those that furthered their own path of self-realization. Bonpos also recognized that we are all capable of achieving our original, pure state through developing awareness, compassion and wisdom.

Today, Bon includes shamanic methods like those described above, as well as a sutra path prescribing moral precepts, a Tantra path using the body and energy to improve health of body and mind, and a Dzogchen[57] path, which teaches how to improve health of body and mind, and how to achieve and abide in the natural state of being.

In Bon, shaman dispel demons and appease the gods, and employ several mudras (ritual postures), mantras (sacred speech), yantras (sacred art) and secret initiation rites.[58]

Modern Bon religion, known as Yungdrung-Bon, and Buddhism are very similar. They embrace many of the same practices and rituals except they have different names or slight variations. Bonpo pilgrims, for example, circumnavigate monuments and mountains and turn prayer wheels counterclockwise rather than clockwise as Buddhists do. They recite the Bon mantra "om matri muye sale du" rather than the Buddhist mantra "om Mani Padme hum." The concepts of karma and rebirth and the six states of existence are featured prominently in Bon as they are in Buddhism. The word Bon sometimes carries with it the same meaning as dharma.

Bon is an ancient religion and philosophy that remains very much alive today. There are Bon monasteries in Tibet and India and many lamas and lay people practise both Buddhism and Bon equally.

Modern Bon is so similar to Buddhism that the Dalai Lama has accepted it as one of the five schools of Tibetan Buddhism.[59]

10.1 Primary Differences Between Buddhism and Bon

Many of the most significant differences are listed below in bullet form: [60]

---

[56]

[57] Wikipedia, "Dzogchen."
[58] BON RELIGION, "Bon Religion, Catholics and Superstition in Tibet."
[59] Ibid.
[60] Tibetan Renaissance Seminar, "Bon Background Research from the Tibetan Renaissance Seminar."

- A counterclockwise circumambulation and eight-syllable mantra instead of six.

- Karma is not as important in Bon, events are occasionally explained by acts of deities and spirits and such.

- Feminine deities play a bigger role, especially in cosmogony.

- Interestingly, however, the relationship between nuns and monks, and the treatment of the former overall, is less progressive than in Buddhism

- Clans remain important, and mitigate the adoption of the incarnate lama strategy.

- Bon rituals established in the canon.

- During the propagation of Bon, temples and stupas were built, but not monasteries, and the propagation was carried out by women and children nearly as much as by men.

- Marriage rituals are more prominent

10.2 Shamanism and Animism

Bon is both a shamanist, and an animist[61] religion.

Shamans have visions and perform various deeds during a trance and it is believed they have power to control spirits in the body. They may leave normal existence and travel or fly to other worlds. Manchu-Tungus nomads of Siberia and northern China language, Shaman means "agitated or frenzied people."

Shaman are bridges between their communities and the spiritual world. During trances, which are induced during a ritual, shaman seek spirits to help cure illnesses, bring about pleasant weather, predict the future, or communicate with deceased ancestors.

Animism attributes a distinct spiritual essence or soul to plants, inanimate objects, and natural phenomena. It is a belief in a supernatural power that organizes and animates the material universe and that ancestors watch over the living from the spirit world.

There are places on earth where sacred power is concentrated. Those places are held sacred and where communication with the spirit world takes place.

---

[61] Wikipedia, "Animism."

10.3 Bon Sarma

Often referred to as New Bon, this is an eclectic tradition combining elements of Indian Buddhism and Yungdrung Bon which appeared in the eighth century AD and is still very popular in eastern Tibet, particularly in Kham.[62]

10.4 Mixed Bon

This refers to the wide range of tribal traditions practised in the borderlands surrounding Tibet and the Himalayas in which Prehistoric Bon, Yungdrung Bon and various other elements mingle in various proportions.[63]

10.5 Bo Murgel

The Bo Murgel belief system of Mongolia and Buryatia—thousands of miles from Tibet—has many features in common with Tibetan Bon, not least of which is its name, Bo—pronounced like "boar" with a double "oar" sound.[64]

10.6 Dzogchen?

Dzogchen or "Great Perfection," it is a tradition of teachings in Tibetan Buddhism aimed at discovering and continuing in the natural primordial state of being. It is a central teaching of the Yungdrung-Bon tradition and in the Nyingma school of Tibetan Buddhism. In these traditions, Dzogchen is the highest and most definitive path of the nine vehicles to liberation.[65] According to this terma, Dzogchen originated with the founder of the Bon tradition, Tonpa Shenrab.

---

[62] Ermakov, "Bo and Bon - Ancient Shamanic Traditions of Siberia and Tibet in Their Relation to the Teachings of a Central Asian Buddha."
[63] Ibid.
[64] Ibid.
[65] Wikipedia, "Dzogchen."

Figure 6. Tibetan Prayer Flags in the colours of the five elements with Mt. Everest

11 Five Spiritual Elements in Tibetan Shamanism

The five elements in Tibetan Shamanism are space, air, fire, water, and earth. In Tibetan philosophy, these elements are symbols of the fundamental forces that compose all phenomenal appearances. These elements create an organized system and are central to most accounts of Tibetan Buddhism.

Tibetan prayer flags are bright and beautiful, but their colours aren't just for show. Each hue signifies an element—and the flags are always arranged in a specific order, from left to right: blue, white, red, green, yellow. Blue represents the sky, white represents the air, red symbolizes fire, green symbolizes water, and yellow symbolizes earth. All five colours together signify balance.[66]

Tibetan Shamanism: Elements & colours	
Space	Blue
Air	White
Fire	Red
Water	Green
Earth	Yellow

A person is a blend of these elements, and to be truly healthy, the energies in these elements need to be balanced in the person.

These five elements—space, air, fire, water, and earth—are symbolic of the fundamental forces that are integral to all phenomena. As the body is developing in the womb, earth provides support, water provides cohesion, fire causes maturing, wind, air cause development, and consciousness, the element of space, provides spaciousness to form the body.

In Tibetan Buddhism and in Tibetan culture, life is seen through these five elements, which continually increase and decrease in relation to one another. This view forms the basis of medicine, astrology, the calendar, and psychology, and it underlies Tibetan traditions of shamanism, Tantra, and Dzogchen.

11.1 Earth

The earth element is the densest expression in form, the most materially present, and is related to qualities of stability, hardness and heaviness.

---

[66] "Prayer Flag."

Find a place where you can be quiet and sit. For myself. This is a favourite bench close to a large lake. The lake will speak to the element of water which comes later. In the warm weather, I will wear sandals and I will take them off and allow my feet to rest on the ground.

Clear your mind of all worries and try to shut out or simply ignore people and even animals around you. Connect and draw from the earth's energy under your feet. I found that even in the cooler fall weather, the ground was "warm" to my bare feet. I also found that pains I had felt in my feet and lower legs went away and stayed away.

This connection to the earth is also known as a grounding exercise. You are grounding yourself and your psyche to something solid, the earth element.

If you cannot find a suitable place to connect with earth, if you have plant pots in which plants are growing, rest your fingertips or your hands on the earth and concentrate on how it feels.

Earth element is stable. Always stable. If you are annoyed or angry at something or someone, focus on the stability of earth's element to reduce and eliminate your anger.

11.2 Water

In my earth exercise, I sat next to a large body of water. Without knowing it, I was completing the water service at the same time as my earth exercise.

While I was fortunate to be close to a large lake, the water in your bath, your shower, or what you drink, sip the water. All will help you feel and understand the water element.

Water, even a glass of water has enormous power. It is cool, and it is warm. It is deep and peaceful until agitated by wind or a spoon stirring in your glass.

Water is the beginning of cohesive form, it is fluid and takes on the shape of any vessel it is in. Place drops of water close to each other on a flat surface, a little movement and the drops will come together and effortlessly combine.

There is no struggle, one drop does not negotiate with another whether they should combine or not and no loss of identity. Two drops simply become one.

Your body is mostly water, connect with the element water, especially that in your own body. If you are in your bath or under your shower, feel how comforting and relaxing it is. If you swim, it will hold you up.

If you are angry or frustrated. Slow down and relax. Let the element of water remove your tensions and take them away. It is comforting, and like earth, it brings stability to you. Be like the water in the container, quiet and passive, allowing the situation to flow over you.

11.3 Fire

The place where I sit with my shows off drinking in the consistency and strength of earth and water also is a very sunny place. I can sit there, close my eyes, feel the earth and listen to the water while the warmth of the sun beams down on me.

In winter, sit before a fire place with a fire burning, if you can. If you cannot burn fuel, a stove, a heater, even your oven while you are cooking is giving off fiery heat—careful not to burn yourself!

Concentrate on the feeling of heat on your face, arms, legs, etc. bring the feeling of heat into your body, through the blood, it flows around the muscles, sinews, ligaments and organs.

In your psyche, fire helps you grow by ripening and maturing your thoughts and feelings. It burns negatives and negativity. Fire speaks to creativity and energetic achievement. Typing on a computer speaks to fire! It brings reality and new interesting things into being.

Fire is also related to digestion and nourishment, the result of which creates the fuel to help your muscles move and stay strong.

If you feel dull, uninspired, listless or unmotivated. Think of the energy of the fire elements and bring it into your body, into your limbs and your intention.

11.4 Air

Air is flowing, movement strength and force. A strong wind that really has no substance can blow over a strong tall tree and a building if it is not built well or insecure.

Again, by the lake where I experience earth, water, and fire, I can also feel wind on my face. It is moving unseen and unheard from the water to the land and yet I feel and sense it.

Think of anger, discomfort, fear, unhappiness, even minor illness such as a headache. Negative thoughts and fears. Those thoughts and fears will make you unhappy, fell down or depressed. Let the wind blow those away and leave your psyche clean, and refreshed.

Air drives sailboats and planes fly on it, and in it. So, do birds and the scent of flowers and seeds seeking a new home in the earth in which to grow.

Air is freedom, flexibility, ease. Let it lift your spirits with the energy and freedom it offers.

Think of air and its ease and internalize it, when you are in a situation that is constricting, limiting, think of air and let it blow those things away and lift your mood and your intention.

11.5 Space

Space is above our heads, we can look up on a clear night and see the stars, the moon, and the space between the stars. Let yourself be open to the wonder you are seeing and relax. Let the infinity of the space you are looking at enter your being and give you a sense of limitlessness.

Space forces open any tight, constricted places inside of you and dissolves away worries. The more and more you integrate with space, the more you are open to opportunities and the bigger your horizons become, you feel less limited or confined.

When you concentrate on space, your mind is clearer, less cluttered, and more energetic. You have less tension; you feel less disrupted. You can sit back and see the big picture and seize the opportunities coming to you because you have more space to accommodate them.

11.6 Imbalance of Elements

Imbalance can manifest itself in the physical dimension. A person with too much earth might be fat or overweight. They may feel devoid of energy and be lazy or depressed.

They may be forgetful, slow, or have very little progression in their personal or spiritual development.

The imbalance of the elements from the Dzogchen perspective is subtler. A person may lack of stability in meditation, lack awareness of their connection to the base, lack of concentration, lack of understanding of Sunyata.

Maybe a person is very unbalanced about the elements in Dzogchen, but he or she might not notice it because there's nothing particularly wrong physically or psychologically.

The Shaman

If you often feel confused or encounter problems, it may be a lack of stabilizing earth. A lack of creativity means you are lacking fire. A lack of openness if you feel as if life is stopping you from speaking up is a lack of space. Someone who is inflexible lacks air.

Too much of any one element can cause problems. Look at the kinds of qualities you are giving to others and your own situation. At those times, look within yourself to get a deeper understanding of the emotional level.

Figure 7. Stupas painted in colours of three of the five elements

11.7 Cause

At birth, we have a good sense of balance in the five elements. Life, as they say, takes its toll. We have so many experiences, some bad, some good. There are so many and some are intense, others not so much. But with so many, we do not always process the experiences and we may become overwhelmed or a tragic event just can't be stopped from leaving poorly grounded.

If you have a profound experience and your sense of balance is equally strong, you will deal with it and remain in balance. Being able to process means, you can feel it anyway, but it will not damage you. It will not change you. It will not weaken you. It will not make you lose some qualities. Being able to process means it will energize you. You are clear about it. In some sense, it can make you grow, make you expand your consciousness, make you become wiser and more understanding.

Not being able to process a shocking event will shake you. If you are a healthy person and you are hit by that experience. Maybe you were happy; when you face it, it will take your happiness away. Somehow, it will damage that quality.

The five negative emotions of anger, desire, ignorance, jealousy, and pride are related to the elements, too. Anger is related to air. Desire is related to white, and so on. When one is more balanced, one can have more experiences with love.

When one is unbalanced because of too much air and lack of earth or grounding, one can have an experience of anger instead. Anger feels like an explosion outward, like air blowing things away—you lose control. This is opposite the experience of when you get depressed, because of too much earth and not enough air.

Figure 8. North American Medicine Wheel

12 Shaman V's a Medicine Man?

A medicine man or medicine woman, there is no gender restriction, is a traditional healer and spiritual leader who serves a community of indigenous people of the Americas. Each culture uses their own name, in their respective Indigenous languages, for the spiritual healers and ceremonial leaders in their particular cultures. [67]

In indigenous North American communities, "medicine" usually refers to spiritual healing. This should not be confused with practitioners who employ Native American ethnobotany, a practice that is very common in many Native American and First Nations households.

Ethnobotany is the study of a region's plants and their practical uses through the traditional knowledge of a local culture and people. An ethnobotanist strives to document the local customs involving the practical uses of local flora for many aspects of life, such as plants as medicines, food, and clothing.[68]

A medicine man or woman usually caries a small pouch that contains sacred items. A personal medicine bag may contain objects that symbolize personal well-being and tribal identity. [1][2] Traditionally, medicine bags are worn under the clothing. [3] Their contents are private, and often of a personal and religious nature.[4] [69]

Other terms for Medicine Man/Woman are "medicine people" or "ceremonial people" are sometimes used in Native American and First Nations communities, for example, when Arwen Nuttall (Cherokee) of the National Museum of the American Indian writes, "The knowledge possessed by medicine people is privileged, and it often remains in particular families." [70]

Native American indigenous people are reluctant to discuss issues about medicine or medicine people with non-Indians. And, in some cultures, the people will not even discuss these matters with members of other tribes. In most tribes, medicine elders are prohibited from advertising or introducing themselves. As Nuttall writes, "An inquiry to a Native person about religious beliefs or ceremonies is often viewed with suspicion."[71]

One example of this is the Apache medicine cord or Izze-kloth whose purpose and use by Apache medicine elders were a mystery to nineteenth-century ethnologists because "the

---

[67] "Medicine Man."
[68] "Ethnobotany."
[69]
[70] THE NATIONAL MUSEUM OF THE AMERICAN INDIAN, "Do All Indians Live in Tipis?."
[71] Ibid.

Apache look upon these cords as so sacred that strangers may not see them, much less handle them or talk about them." [72]

The term "medicine man/woman," like the term "shaman," has been criticized by Native Americans, as well as other specialists in the fields of religion and anthropology. [73]

While non-Native anthropologists sometimes use the term "shaman" for Indigenous healers worldwide, including the Americas, "shaman" is the specific name for a spiritual mediator from the Tungstic peoples of Siberia and is not used in Native American or First Nations communities. [74]

The term "medicine man/woman" has also frequently been used by Europeans to refer to African traditional healers, along with the offensive term "witch doctors." [75] The term "witch doctor is also considered having a negative connotation, or, its use should belittle or disparage.

A medicine man, or woman's approach to sickness, disease or misfortune, is to strive to discover the root causes and divine how to prevent the symptoms and conditions from recurring. Rather than the symptom/cure-based approach of modern medicine. They do this by exploring the supernatural causes of ill health.

There is great emphasis on medicinal plants to heal colds, cough, fever, asthma, and insect bites. A medicine man/woman is a person with mysterious power over medicine or magic or other mysterious arts. The individual knows that some medicine is good in treating an illness, some evil or bad. Bad medicine may be infective, or make the condition worse.[76] It might also be poisonous.

Of all the African religious specialists, medicine-men were the most useful, and people consult them frequently. They acted as the link between the people and the supernatural realm. Africans believe the cause of ill health, misfortunes and other afflictions could be traced to the invisible world. Since most of the people could not communicate with the forces that controlled that world, the medicine-men became very useful (Magesa 1997,210). [77]

---

[72] "Annual Report of the Bureau of American Ethnology to the Secretary of the… Pdf," *Smithsonian Institution. Bureau of American Ethnology.*
[73] Wikipedia, "Medicine Man."
[74] Drake Eastburn, "Healer, Shaman, Facilitator," *International Journal of Complementary & Alternative Medicine* 5, no. 2 (2017).
[75] Ibid.
[76] Peter M. Mumo, "Holistic Healing, an Analytical Review of Medicine-Men in African Societies."
[77] Ibid.

The Shaman

As with other specialists in African Religion, medicine-men/women receive a calling to the profession. Africans believe some were born with the ability, having been born holding divination pebbles. The midwives would note relevant signs and inform the mothers that they had special children. In other cases, a medicine-man would pass on the profession to his son or other younger relative (Mbiti 1969, 167). Others received their calls through visions or dreams (Magesa1997,217). In addition, upcoming medicine—men went through training that involved attachment to practising medicine-men. The trainees learned the several ways available of dealing with health issues. Africans believed that medicine men possessed special gifts or powers (Magesa 1997, 219). Through training they were shown how to use those gifts and powers. After training, they were officially installed through a ceremony presided over by a medicine-man.[78]

The cleansing rituals that followed marked a new start in life, symbolized by shaving the hair, lighting a new fire, or sweeping the house ceremoniously. Such rituals may not mean much to an observer… They are psychologically vital and, no doubt play a significant role in healing the sick or helping the sufferer (Ndung'u and Mwaura 2008, 45).[79]

Both Christianity and colonialism in Africa have sought to discredit African psychological healing, which involves promoting the mental and emotional well-being of the individual and the techniques developed for psychological healing is developed in an African environment to address specific problems. Some Africans afflicted by certain crises can only be addressed using this approach. These afflictions include barrenness, mental disturbances, misfortunes and effects of witchcraft and sorcery in humans, combined with unproductive farms and animals (Mumo2009, 63). [80]

Comparing a shaman to a medicine man or woman there are some notable differences. The shaman soul journeys either for themselves or at the request of another for healing purposes. A soul journey may also be undertaken to retrieve a soul or to help guide a lost spirit or a spirit that has not crossed over into the spirit world. Battles and confrontations with evil or dark spirits and souls may help a sick individual. The shaman's universe includes an upper, middle and lower realm where spirits exist, along with the spirits of ancestors who must be understood and persuaded to help a soul in its current physical incarnation.

A shaman experiences possession by a spirit guide during a healing ceremony. It is also the case that a spirit guide may be human or animal, but it is a guide they are familiar with and have a close relationship with.

---

[78] Ibid.
[79] Ibid.
[80] Ibid.

The Shaman

A shaman, especially one from Mongolia and Tibet, does minor work regarding herbs and natural herbal treatments.

The Shaman

Figure 9. Closeup of a witch from an indigenous African tribe

13   Shaman V's a Witch Doctor?

The word 'witchcraft' elicits the worst stereotypical, virulent, and extremely negative images in most people's minds. There is almost a conditioned reflex of the word. The term automatically evokes and reinforces images of 'ignorance,' 'backwardness,' 'primitive,' 'uncivilized,' 'superstitious,' 'undeveloped.' It confirms deeply ingrained negative opinions of the society and the individuals who are known as Witch doctors.

A witch doctor was originally a type of healer who treated ailments believed to be caused by witchcraft. The term witch doctor is sometimes used to refer to healers, particularly in regions which use traditional healing rather than contemporary medicine.[81]

In its original meaning, witch doctors were emphatically not witch's themselves, but people who had remedies to protect others against witchcraft. Within their tribe or community, a witch doctor was a user of magic, who by use of spells, charms, herbal remedies, and incantations sought to cure illness, detect witches, and counteract malevolent magical influences. Witchcraft-induced conditions were their area of expertise.

Since the missionaries thought they were introducing civilization into Africa, they denounced African institutions, including African approaches to healing. They referred to medicine-men and women who were highly respected for their services as 'witch doctors.' On the attitude of Europeans to African healing, Ndung'u and Mwaura explain that 'the whole process of healing was in the eyes of the missionaries, part of a wide scheme of witchcraft and paganism and had to be eradicated in order to pave the way for western civilization and the Gospel' (Ndung'u and Mwaura 2008, 46). [82]

'When people see havoc in medical institutions, the powerlessness of doctors, they go to healers. There's another point, incurable diseases or oncology. When it's a child, they want to turn the world upside down to cure it. So, people go to healers searching for a miracle. This is not about the level of education of those people who go to healers, but about the level of trust in the medicine offered by the state,'[83]

Whilst no one deny that the tribes throughout Africa. As a whole, believe in witchcraft, it does not follow that the witch doctor himself is feared, or that he is the evil person who many people depict him to be. Indeed, among the Shona people he is a much respected and, I might add,

---

[81] Wikipedia, "Witch Doctor."
[82] Mumo, "Holistic Healing, an Analytical Review of Medicine-Men in African Societies."
[83] Dinara. Director Alyaeva, Pomogat Legko, Russia, Interview.

much beloved person, and—if I may be permitted to make the comparison—he is even regarded with the same attachment that the doctor enjoys in European society.[84]

Most Africans' belief\'e will the existence of the witch, and to most people, the witch denotes a person with an evil spirit capable of causing untold misery, tragedy and death upon any innocent victim. Again, to the Shona people the witch, like the witch doctor, is spiritually endowed. But with a spirit which operates against the interests of humankind. The witch, like the witch doctor, also inherits a spirit from the mother, and this trait is handed down in the family. The witch practices witchcraft and can manipulate occult forces to the detriment of man—quite the opposite to the witch doctor, who operates the forces for the good of humanity. Thus, the only difference really between the witch doctor and the witch is the eternal difference of good and bad.[85]

The fountainhead of the belief in magic and witchcraft is the witch doctor, and the continuance of this philosophy rests on him. As long as he exists, so long can we accept hi" presence as the sign of his people's belief and dependence on magic and witchcraft. Once he goes, this extraordinary ancient philosophy will disappear as well.

The witch doctor's functions thus extend far beyond the mere prescribing of a herb albeit this be an important aspect of his practice. He is the hub around which the magical or spiritual world revolves, giving succour and support to those in need and being the means of ensuring good behaviour.[86]

The roles of the witch doctor differ from the Shaman in this context and are reliant on the existence of a witch, someone who communicates with the spirit world to do harm to others. As with the Medicine Man/Woman, described earlier, many of the attributes of the shaman are not present when discussing witch doctors.

Interestingly, the men and women in Europe recognized as white witches who practise witchcraft. The only difference from the witch discussed here is that a white witch serves the people and is much sought after to cure their diseases. Therefore, the white witch really corresponds to the African witch doctor and there is no difference between the witch doctor and the witch except in their handling of the powers of Nature.[87]

---

[84] MICHAEL GELFAND, "Medicine and Magic," *The Central African Journal of Medicine*.
[85] Ibid.
[86] Ibid.
[87] ibid.

Figure 10. Tibetan Shaman in full Costume, Drumming and Dancing

14 Shamanism: Rituals and Spirituality

Shamanism is universal and not bound by social or cultural conditions. It is the most ancient and most enduring spiritual tradition known to humanity. Shamanism predates and makes up the foundation of all known religions or religious philosophies.[88]

In the Shaman's world view, spirits and demons inhabit everything around us. Every part of the natural environment is alive with different sentient forces. Literally, the world is alive, in the mountains, trees, rivers and lakes, rocks, fields, the sky, and the earth. There are supernatural spirits and souls. Added to this, each region has its own native spiritual beings, and people living in those areas are powerfully aware of their presence. In order to stay in the spirit's good graces, offerings are made, rituals performed and sometimes people will refrain from particular places to avoid the more dangerous forces.

The focus of Buddhist teaching and practice is centred on commonplace goals, seeking advice from shamans whose function is to contact spirits, to predict their influences on people's lives, and to perform rituals that either overcome harmful influences or otherwise ask for their help makes sense. Making such request and receiving a shaman's aid should give people a measure of control over their unpredictable lives and surroundings.

Rituals conducted today have changed from those of previous centuries. Not that they are any less effective today, they are. But the style and form of them from previous centuries have changed. Comparing rituals and practices from previous generations or those performed centuries ago to today makes little sense.

When Tonpa Shenrab came to Tibet which, according to the well-known 20th-century Buddhist scholar Gedun Chophel he blessed Tibet and its people, sharing many teachings, ceremonies and religious dances that are distinctly Bon. The most important change he introduced was to eliminate animal sacrifices. The local practice was to sacrifice animals in order to appease spirits responsible for causing sickness and misfortune. Tonpa Shenrab taught them they could offer red torma and white torma in place of animals. Torma is figures made mostly of flour and butter used in tantric rituals or as offerings in Tibetan Buddhism. They may be dyed in different colours, often with white or red for the main body of the torma. They are made in specific shapes based on their purpose, usually conical in form.[89] In this way, Tonpa Shenrab established the peaceful enlightened Yungdrung-Bon tradition.[90]

---

[88] shamanicdrumming.com, "Shamanic Drumming."
[89] Wikipedia, "Torma."
[90] buddhaweekly.com/, "Iinterview-Bon-Teacher-Chaphur-Rinpoche-Explains-Bon-Different-Similar-Five-Buddhist-Schools-Tibet."

The Shaman

The Shaman is contemporary to the world they live in. They wear clothes and use tools and aids suitable to the society and expectations of their clients. To bring "bear" energy to his or her client the shaman may wear something to connect with that animal or spirits energy. A bear claw beneath the shirt or wrap a subtle piece of fur around their rattle handle would be acceptable.

The shaman believes they are talking to guides, perhaps spirits and those spirits can help them heal. In order to heal, the shaman must be able to connect with the recipient of the healing. This means the recipient of healing needs to be open to receiving it.

If a shaman hasn't aligned with practices and rituals of a particular culture, preferring to belong to the one of their birth, they are considered being contemporary shaman and needs to be authentic and able to communicate this to the recipient and for the information to be accepted.

Direct connection with the spirits is through song and dance. The rhythm of the music, song and dance take the shaman into a state of ecstasy where he, or she, is in direct communion with the spirits, they go beyond ordinary human existence and reach a transcendental state of simultaneous existence in this world and the next, and bring him back with messages and information. They also close the session with the spirits and his souls returns to him.

14.1 Drums and drumstick

Figure 11. Drumming

Usually the shaman's drum is a fixture of their healing ceremonies and has special qualities. It has been blessed by the shaman who owns and uses it only. A spirit may exist in the drum that helps the shaman in releasing part of his soul into the journeys he undertakes when it is used. Drumming has a specific role to play in a ceremony.

A slow repetitive drumming rhythm with a frequency close to that measured from the earth has proved effective for most people. It helps induce a range of ecstatic trance states in order to connect with the spiritual dimension of reality. Practised in diverse cultures around the planet, this drum method is strikingly similar to the world over.

Just the way a soothing song can help an someone achieve a calmer state. The rhythm of the drum puts you in the right state to journey. The drum beat used is very close to the frequency that is measured from the earth, and has proved effective for most people.

As the Shaman transits through different trance states, the drumming rhythm changes. Eventually the shaman reaches the level necessary for healing to take place. The drumming tempo will change and slow down when the shaman preparing to leave the trance state. The change in tempo helps draw their consciousness back to normal.

Power animal drumming is a shamanic way to evoke and internalize animal archetypes. An animal archetype represents the spirit and attributes of the entire species of that animal. Shamanism is the endeavour to cultivate ongoing relationships with power animals to gain insight, healing methods, and other vital information that can benefit the community. When an animal spirit is invoked, there is often an accompanying rhythm that comes through. Shamans frequently use these unique rhythms to summon their helping spirits for the work at hand. [91]

14.2 Songs

The most important thing about a shamanic song is whether it is effective.

The purpose of the shamanic song is to connect to, and bring in different energies. The purpose of the singing that song is to shift one's state of mind and the state of the group that is singing. The song doesn't have to be beautiful, or perfectly written. The power of the song is the doorway that it opens between the shaman or the individuals and the power of the spirit world. That doorway is actually open by the singer(s), not the song itself. Some songs are more effective at helping you open that door.[92]

Shamanic songs can be unique to individual healers and/or groups of people, they really aren't different from any spiritual song. Often, the shaman will go to the spirit world to obtain the lyrics or melody of the song. They may have an occasion or a purpose and they will consult with the spirit world to be inspired by a song that fits well with what they want to do.

In terms of spiritual practice, there are many healthful benefits to singing, and positive purposes for singing. Here are some of those benefits: [93]

- Singing is a very powerful way of filling yourself with good energy.

- Singing can help you change your emotions, or your state of mind.

- Shamans use songs to help groups harmonize their energy with one another.

- Singing can help you connect with a higher power, such as angels, or guardian spirits, or the divine (in whatever way you name it).

---

[91] shamanicdrumming.com, "Shamanic Drumming."
[92] shamanlinks.net, "Singing Shamanic Songs - Shaman Links."
[93] Ibid.

- You can use singing to bring good energy into a room. In some spiritual practices, songs are used to invoke or invite. For instance, there are songs for rain, or songs for inviting a power animal to be with you.

- Many shamans have a healing song that they sing when they work with their clients.

- Songs can be used to bless another person or a group of people.

- Singing can connect you to the deeper knowing that is inside of you.

- Songs can help you release or express feelings or stuck energies you have found it difficult to release or express by thinking or talking about them.

- Songs are capable of healing you.

14.3 Dance

Dance is a creative activity. A shaman will add dance to their drumming and singing to bring spirits into our world. These are spirits they have asked their helping spirits to bring for the purposes of healing. Physically moving the human body requires energy, coordination and strongly reinforces the request and connection. It adds a mutual energy exchange between the shaman and the spirits they are dancing with.

When the spirit is an animal, certain steps and actions during the dance will mimic and imply the spirit of the animal the shaman is connected with.

Dance is also a traditional element of spiritual practice. The intention and form of the dance may have a specific purpose. A dance may start as a method of connecting to and invoking spirits for the healing that is requested. Later, towards the end of the dance, the message to the spirits maybe one of thanks for attending and participating in the ceremony.

Some shaman will dance because they enjoy dancing with their spirits and guides and this personal connection through motion and energy is an important way to express and enjoy their connection.

14.4 Costumes

All parts of the costume are personal to the shaman. A shaman's costume is not bought off the shelf, it is made on the direction of the spirits and the spirit world the shaman journeys to. It is made of time and may have things added to it and taken away depending on the humanizing the shaman is undertaking.

The other aspect of the costume is the self-training wearing the costume instill on the shaman. By putting on the costume, they are communicating to themselves the role they are taking on, the power they are seeking to accept and connect with and also the start of the session. By taking it off, they are leaving the session and the connection.

14.5 Head Band and Head Dress

Feathers symbolize flight, travel, and the ability of the shaman to travel with and to the spirits he or she must visit in the upper or lower worlds to discover the cause of what is afflicting the recipient and how healing is to be achieved. Feathers from powerful birds, especially predators such as Eagles instill power into the headdress and the shaman's connection to these animals.

If the shaman's power animal is a bird, feathers or claws of the bird are an essential part of the headdress and show honour and the state of their connectedness because the shaman is wearing aspects of the physical animal.

Other symbolize can be communicated in the head dress. The four seasons, the four directions certain elements. Parts of the Shamanic cosmos can also appear. Even the DNA spiral can be added to a modern shaman's head dress and head band.

A head band may have cords or tassels hanging down which cover the face and form a screen which prevents people from seeing the shaman's face. There are three reasons usually offered for this:

1. The shaman will take on the characteristics of their helping spirit or guide. This may include the face of a guide that has long since passed over. People seeing this altered face would/might be scared. The screen hides the face of the spirit from onlookers.

2. The cords and tassels symbolize the nature of the two worlds. The physical world is on our side of the cord screen, the shaman, is on the other side, soul journeying in another realm.

3. Distraction. The screen removes the physical world from the shaman's gaze, removing what is taking place around him, allowing him to blend and connect with the spirit world more effectively.

The Shaman

Figure 12. A Shaman

14.6 Cloak

As with the head dress and head band, there are no strict guidelines on how to build and what should be represented on such a shamanic garment. It should include more connections to their power animal and spirits they are connected with. This may mean duplicating some aspects of the head dress and head band, but reinforcement of these helping spirits is very acceptable.

They are allies and helpers in the spirit world, expressing the connection cannot be done too often!

The cloak also represents energy, a shield against harmful or malevolent spirits the shaman may encounter. Some shaman, at the direction of their helping spirits may attach panels of highly polished metal to their cloak. The metal acts as a mirror.

A malevolent spirit seeking to attack the shaman will see themselves in the mirror and become confused and leave. Metal is used, because a piece of an actual mirror may break and become useless. Shards of glass are also dangerous to the shaman if the malevolent spirt finds a way to use a piece to attack the shaman. Bells and metal made to rattle can be attached to scare away harmful spirits.

14.7 Foot Wear

During shamanizing, dancing, and soul journeying, strong, protective footwear is required! Footwear, usually some sort of boots can be decorated with symbols and elements of power animals, helping spirits and guides. Something along the lines of these boots will bring me home. But also, if during a soul journey the shaman must cross a river, walk on water, or across rough ground, suitable footwear is required.

14.8 Alters and Shrines

Alters and shrines in a home or shamanic place of healing reinforce the shamans power animal, and all helping spirits. Metal mirrors may be on display to ward off and confuse any dark or lower spirits which may seek to harm the shaman as he prays.

Members of the shaman's family may be represented, especially if those family members were shamans, their energy and strength can be called on to help the living shaman. Food offering and offerings of other acceptable gifts to the spirits will be displayed and available for the spirits to consume.

The Shaman

Representation of local spirits associated with the spiritual beings of the area where the shaman is living will be important. When humans build houses or even set down a temporary abode, we disrupt the spirits in the local area. By showing them on the altar, we honour them and ask for their agreement to us staying there.

Figure 13. S. Korean Mudang, Shaman. Ecstasy in Dance

14.9 Modern Korea and Shamanism

Korean Shamanism is one of several religions in Korea but the only native belief system to the peninsula. The shamanism predates Buddhism, Confucianism, Taoism and Christianity in general but in Korea it has proved to be surprisingly adaptable to Korea's modern industrial society. It is not gender specific though the majority of the shaman in Korea are female.

It is important to remember that religion in Korea and much of East Asia is not a "sum-zero" game but rather people will maintain traditions from more than one religion and philosophy.

One does not need to identify themselves as a follower of shamanism to ask for a shaman's help.

Korean shamanism has much in common with shamanism in northern Asia including Siberia.

Korean shamans, sing and dance during their rituals some songs, known as the muga, are invocations and prayers, while others explain the origins of the various gods. These narrative muga are often quite long and may take hours to sing in their entirety.

A Korean shamanic ritual is called a Kut. Music drummed and sung is the most important part of the ritual and as mentioned before it helps the mudang, Korean shaman, reach a trance state. In the past decades, changes in the music and song have indicated to the audience, change in the ritual. But as these ceremonies and rituals are becoming increasingly entertainment focused. A drummer and symbolic weapons like swords and tridents are used during the ceremony. Changes in music and song are inevitably used for entertainment purposes.

In Korea today, there are musicians, called aksas, who create ensembles especially for a Kut. Most mudang can play many instruments and sing all the songs needed for their ceremonies. The Korean mudang has become a professional musician and who represents a feature that is to Korean shamanism. Inevitably, for entertainment purposes, musicians, lighting and other specialists have become engaged in presenting a staging a performance, something very different from the Siberian and Tibetan Shaman who do not use these specialists.

The mudang is chosen to fill a role of mediating between spirits and human and perform healing ceremonies. There are no special powers processed by the mudang, all their power comes from eth spirits they work with and through her. There is no intrinsic power in the shaman's words or deeds, they acquire their force from the shaman's skill as a medium, messenger, and mediator.

The Shaman

A mudang often begins her practice with very little of the paraphernalia necessary for carrying out an extensive Kut. As she practises her art, she acquires patrons or tan'gol who over the lifetime of her practice eventually supply her with the necessary tools of her trade. She must acquire numerous costumes, altar paraphernalia, musical instruments, and other props for the Kut.

Until recently Korean shamanism was oral tradition in a society where Confucian and Buddhist literature and written liturgies abounded.

What is important to note is that apart from the modern shaman's associations, religious practices have taken place among rather loosely connected groups of mudangs or in a hereditary shaman family. There is very little institutionalization or development of canonical texts that would lead to standardization. Uniformity among Korean shamans is more a matter of cooperation and tradition rather than coercion. Cooperation is usually quite good, but occasionally rivalries do develop on a personal level between shamans.

For a detailed paper on Muga and Kuts in Korean Shamanism.

Please refer to:

- The Use of Muga in Korean Shaman Kuts a Case Study for the Application of Performative Language Theory in Cross Culture Hermeneutics by James Ware, Austin College.

The Shaman

Figure 14. Shaman Messages on the wind

15 Shamanism: Changing Perceptions

As noted in the sections on Witch Doctors and Medicine People, they are *not* shaman, calling any other indigenous traditional healer a shaman is also not correct. The shamans discussed and their heritage is in Tibet, Nepal, and on the Mongolian Plain as well as Siberia.

In those regions the shamans have filled many roles through history. In their societies, they have been a traditionally healer, spiritual leader, ritualist, soul guide, sacrificer, song reciter, dancer, and dramatic performer, confident and even a tribal leader.

In a trance they would journey to other realms, sometimes dangerous and threatening realms. On those journeys they were guided by spirits and animals, they retrieved souls that had become lost or even stolen. They journeys to find and discover the cause of illness and how to remedy and heal the recipient.

These abilities, ceremonies and paraphernalia have made shaman targets for persecution and mistreatment as "modern" western religions connected with shamans. Drums, ceremonial clothing and all evidence of the shaman's ability were burned and destroyed, baptism was enforced.

Perhaps worse, denigration of shamans as lesser people, themselves by calling they by disrespectful names and labels such as devils, demons, and assigning them a lower rank or status in society.

The twentieth century misapplication of the word shaman to other cultural heritages denigrates the word and the societies to which it rightfully applies as well as those it does not.

Persecution of Siberian shamans and prohibition of shamanic ceremonies began in 17th century Siberia at the time orthodox Christianity was forced on eth population. Yet, it failed to eradicate shamanism, many Russians, even czarist officials, turned to shamanic practitioners for the advice and assistance and availed themselves of the shaman's otherworldly capabilities.

Declining religious influence, especially Judo-Christian churches in the Western world has coincided with the realignment of shamanism by scientific investigation and reporting who now see the shaman as a neuropsychiatric healer.

During a shamanic ceremony, the shaman will enter an altered state of consciousness [ASC]. The ASC is often referred to as an ecstatic state. It is during this time that they connect with the other realms they are journeying to, their helping spirits and the gods and spirits that will help them, help the recipient, on whose behalf they are making this journey.

The ecstatic state also describes a dislocation between the physical individual that is the shaman in the ceremony and the soul of a person journeying to another realm. Another way to think of this is the Out of Body experience commonly reported by many people. In an out-of-body experience their two souls or beings exist, the physical one and the ephemeral one that can journey across the room, look at a room from a different perspective or across the world. Military forces, notably the US and Russians have experimented with "remote viewing" as they describe it for decades.

In shamanic ceremonies the ASC state is self-induced by the shaman and western medical background have frequently attributed psychopathology from actions and expressions of shamanic practitioners in such an ASC; of shaman candidates during their initiatory period and of performing shamans during their ceremonies.

Most traditional non-Western cultures and in historical European cultures, ASC are or were interpreted either as a special state of the individual permitting of close interaction with supernatural entities, in order to receive their messages, perceive them in visions, and acquire power from them; or, as a state of possession in which a supernatural entity or power acts through the individual.[94]

It is worth noting at this point that the shaman is not possessed. Shamanism is not a possession state belief. Shamanic possession is not actually possession at all, but the intentional embodiment of spirit help with whom the shaman has already developed a working relationship. Possession is unintentional intrusion of a foreign spirit into a person who is considered an energetic illness or unhealthy state in shamanism. Embodiment is an effective, working, altered state the shaman is able to begin and end at will.

Shamanism and possession nonetheless share biological features in their elicitation of ancient brain systems to modify the consciousness in relation to healing and spiritual experiences.

Shamans are chosen by a spirit, or the demonstrate the ability to connect with the other realms and spirits but have no reference to do so and no way of organizing and managing what is happening to them. This is not a role people can vie for like a class president. There is no written exam mark to be passed. The initiatory sickness as it is called takes many forms depending on the person being called and their circumstances. Nervous fits, attacks of insanity, loss of consciousness, epileptic convulsions and experiences of being torn apart or dismembered are some of them. In the 2000s the experience and reference points will be different from those of hundreds of years ago. Recovery from the sickness is presented by

---

[94] Wolfgang G. Jilek, "Transforming the Shaman Changing Western Views of Shamanism and Altered States of Consciousness."

shaman teachers as a form of death and rebirth; being reborn to the shamanic vocation as a changed person.[95]

On the individual and interpersonal level, shamanic practitioners, unlike Western-trained health professionals, combine the confidence-inspiring reputation of a charismatic personality with access to supernatural powers and a culture-congenial understanding of their clients' belief and value system. [96]

All this may explain the survival of shamanic practices among indigenous peoples in spite of centuries of suppression by governmental and ecclesiastical authorities. However, beyond mere survival we witness a revival of shamanic healing rituals and ceremonialism, especially among North American indigenous populations under Westernizing acculturation pressure. This indigenous renaissance is reflected in the revitalization of traditional ceremonials with important therapeutic aspects, throughout North America.

Examples are the Winter Spirit Dances of the Salish in the Pacific Northwest; the Sun Dance among aboriginal populations of Wyoming, Idaho, Utah, Colorado, and the Dakotas; the Gourd Dance among the Kiowa, Comanche, Cheyenne, and Arapaho, which subsequently reached many other tribes in the United States and Canada; the Peyote Cult which spread northward from Mexico and is today a major pan-Amerindian religious ceremonial east of the Rocky Mountains. [97]

In North America, the expansion of rituals and ceremonies speaks to the need for indigenous people to have an identity unique and special to themselves. Preserving and expanding the role of traditional healers is a powerful way of expressing this voice while allowing for modern medicine to intervene where necessary.

In reading and exploring the role of Tibetan Shaman, and Shamanism at the roof of the world. Shaman there do not diagnose and will send a potential client to a doctor to get antibiotics or more expensive treatment.

Beginning in the later part of the 1900s what we call "New Age" shamanism, has appeared and taken hold in people and places without the indigenous or traditional heritage associated with shamanism.

This profound and honest interest in shamanism in cultures that do not have a historical connection to shamanism is due to an inquiring mind and desire to understand and the feeling

---

[95] Ibid.
[96] Ibid.
[97] Ibid.

that there is more to what I know and understand. Shamanism would not have survived from the Paleolithic without it having substance to it.

The revival of shamanic ceremonialism is one aspect of the renaissance of indigenous culture. It is no coincidence this occurred in the aftermath of decolonization, accompanied by a profound change of the prevailing Western attitudes after World War II. There has been a change in the world view and sense of superiority. No longer are Europe or North America the centre for everything that is right and correct, and prepared to remake everything in their image. Today they are the source of financial resources, powerful inquisitiveness, and a desire to explore and understand.

Figure 15. Sacred Mount Kailash

16 Sacred Places in Tibet

16.1 Mount Kailash

The mountain is located near Lake Manasarovar and Lake Rakshastal, close to the source of some of the longest Asian rivers: the Indus, Sutlej, Brahmaputra, and Karnali also known as Ghaghara (a tributary of the Ganges) in India.[98]

A great mass of black rock soaring to over 22,000 feet, Mt. Kailash has the unique distinction of being the world's most venerated holy place while it is the least visited. The supremely sacred site of four religions and billions of people, Mt. Kailash is seen by no more than a few thousand pilgrims each year. This curious fact is explained by the mountain's remote location in far western Tibet. No planes, trains or buses journey anywhere near the region and even with rugged overland vehicles the journey still requires weeks of difficult, often dangerous travel. The weather, always cold, can be unexpectedly treacherous and pilgrims must carry all the supplies they will need for the entire journey.[99]

The cosmologies and origin myths of each of these religions speak of Mt. Kailash as the mythical Mt. Meru, the Axis Mundi, the centre and birth place of the entire world. The mountain was already legendary before the great Hindu epics, the Ramayana and the Mahabharata, were written. Indeed, Kailash is so deeply embedded in the myths of ancient Asia that it was perhaps a sacred place of another era, another civilization, now long gone and forgotten.

For Tibetans, pilgrimage refers to the journey from ignorance to enlightenment, from self-centredness and materialistic preoccupations to a deep sense of the relativity and interconnectedness of all life. The Tibetan word for pilgrimage, neykhor, means "to circle around a sacred place," for the goal of pilgrimage is less to reach a destination than to transcend through inspired travel the attachments and habits of inattention that restrict awareness of a larger reality.[100]

16.2 Bon

Bon, a religion native to Tibet, maintain that the entire mystical region and Kailash, which they call the "nine-story Swastika Mountain," is the axis mundi, Tagzig Olmo Lung Ring.

---

[98] Wikipedia, "Mount Kailash."
[99] Sacredsites.com, "World Pilgrimigae Guide."
[100] Ibid.

The great Vajrayana sage, Milarepa, seeking to establish Buddhism in Tibet engaged in a magical battle with the Bon shaman, Naro-Bon-Chung to win the heart of the Tibetan people. It is said they battled for many days with no clear victor. The final and decisive stage of the battle was a race to the top of Mount Kailash, the same mountain associated with Shiva. Milarepa won, but in a gesture of generosity and compassion tossed a snowball to Naro-Bon-Chung. A gesture understood to symbolize the syncretic integration of the new dispensation of Buddhism with the old shamanic Bon tradition. There could hardly be a more perfect expression of the Archangel Zadkiel's righteous compassion and sense of justice that transcends ego.[101]

16.3 Hindus

Hindus believe Mt. Kailash to be the abode of Lord Shiva. Like many of the Hindu gods, Shiva is a character of apparent contradictions. He at once the Lord of Yoga and therefore the ultimate renunciate ascetic, yet he is also the divine master of Tantra, the esoteric science that regards sexual union as the most perfect path to spiritual enlightenment. According to legend, immortal Shiva lives atop Kailash where he spends his time practising yogic austerities, making joyous love with his divine consort, Parvati, and smoking ganja, the sacred herb known in the west as marijuana, Hindus do not interpret Shiva's behaviours as contradictory, however, but rather see in him a deity who has wisely integrated the extremes of human nature and thus transcended attachment to any particular, and limited, way of being. For a Hindu, to make the arduous pilgrimage to Kailash and have the darshan (divine view) of Shiva's abode is to obtain release from the clutches of ignorance and delusion. [102]

16.4 Jains

Mt. Kailash is sacred to other religions as well. The Jains call the mountain Astapada and believe it to be the place where Rishaba, the first of the twenty-four Tirthankaras attained liberation. Followers of Bon, Tibet's pre-Buddhist, shamanistic religion, call the mountain Tise and believe it to be the seat of the Sky Goddess Sipaimen. Additionally, Bon myths regard Tise as the sight of a legendary 12th-century battle of sorcery between the Buddhist sage Milarepa and the Bon shaman Naro Bon-Chung. Milarepa's defeat of the shaman displaced Bon as the primary religion of Tibet, firmly establishing Buddhism in its place. While the Buddha is believed to have magically visited Kailash in the fifth century BC, the religion of Buddhism only entered Tibet, via Nepal and India, in the seventh century AD. Tibetan Buddhists call the

---

[101] wingsofchaos.com, "Prologue for Zadkiel."
[102] Sacredsites.com, "World Pilgrimigae Guide."

mountain Kang Rimpoche, the "Precious One of Glacial Snow," and regard it as the dwelling place of Demchog (also known as Chakrasamvara) and his consort, Dorje Phagmo. Three hills rising near Kang Rimpoche are believed to be the homes of the Bodhisattvas Manjushri, Vajrapani, and Avalokiteshvara.

After the difficult journey getting to Mt. Kailash, they are confronted by the arduous task of circumambulating the sacred peak. This walking around the mountain (clockwise for the Buddhists, counter-clockwise for Bon adherents) is known as a Kora, or Parikrama, and normally takes three days.

In hopes of gaining extra merit or psychic powers, however, some pilgrims will vary the tempo of their movement. A hardy few, practising a secret breathing technique known as Lung-gom, will power themselves around the mountain in only one day. Others will take two to three weeks for the kora by making full-body prostration the entire way. It is believed that a pilgrim who completes 108 journeys around the mountain is assured enlightenment. Most pilgrims to Kailash will also take a short plunge in the nearby, highly sacred (and very cold) Lake Manosaravar. The word "manas" means mind or consciousness; the name Manosaravar means Lake of Consciousness and Enlightenment. Adjacent to Manosaravar is Rakas Tal or Rakshas, the Lake of Demons. Pilgrimage to this great sacred mountain and these two magical lakes is a life-changing experience and an opportunity to view some of the most magical scenery on the entire planet.

Figure 16. Tibetan Buddhist Monestary

16.5 Potala Palace:

The Potala Palace is a dzong fortress in the city of Lhasa, in China's Tibet Autonomous Region. It was the winter palace of the Dalai Lamas from 1649 to 1959, has been a museum since then, and is a World Heritage Site since 1994. [103]

The site on which the Potala Palace rises is built over a palace erected by Songtsen Gampo on the Red Hill. The Potala contains two chapels on its northwest corner that conserve parts of the original building. One is the Phakpa Lhakhang, the other the Chogyel Drupuk, a recessed cavern identified as Songtsen Gampo's meditation cave.

Lozang Gyatso, the Great Fifth Dalai Lama, started the construction of the modern Potala Palace in 1645 after one of his spiritual advisers, Konchog Chophel (died 1646), pointed out that the site was ideal as a seat of government, situated as it is between Drepung and Sera monasteries and the old city of Lhasa. The external structure was built in 3 years, while the interior, together with its furnishings, took 45 years to complete.

The Dalai Lama and his government moved into the Potrang Karpo ("White Palace") in 1649. Construction lasted until 1694, some twelve years after his death. The Potala was used as a winter palace by the Dalai Lama from that time. The Potrang Marpo ("Red Palace") was added between 1690 and 1694.

---

[103] Wikipedia, "Potala Palace."

Figure 17. Potala Palace

16.6 Jokhang Temple

Figure 18. Jokhang Temple

Jokhang Temple is a Buddhist temple.

The Jokhang was founded during the reign of King Songtsen Gampo. According to tradition, the temple was built for the king's two brides: Princess Wencheng of the Chinese Tang dynasty and Princess Bhrikuti of Nepal. Both are said to have brought important Buddhist statues and images from China and Nepal to Tibet, which were housed here, as part of their dowries. The oldest part of the temple was built in 652. Over the next 900 years, the temple was enlarged several times with the last renovation done in 1610 by the Fifth Dalai Lama. Following the death of Gampo, the image in Ramcho Lake temple was moved to the Jokhang temple for security reasons. When King Tresang Detsen ruled from 755 to 797, the Buddha image of the Jokhang temple was hidden, as the king's minister was hostile to the spread of Buddhism in Tibet. During the late ninth and early tenth centuries, the Jokhang and Ramoche temples were said to have been used as stables. In 1049 Atisha, a renowned teacher of Buddhism from Bengal taught in Jokhang.[104]

Tibetans viewed their country as a living entity controlled by srin ma (pronounced "sinma"), a wild demoness who opposed the propagation of Buddhism in the country. To thwart her evil intentions, King Songtsen Gampo, the first king of a unified Tibet, developed a plan to build twelve temples across the country. The temples were built in three stages. In the first stage, central Tibet was covered with four temples, known as the "four horns" (ru bzhi). Four more temples (mtha'dul), were built in the outer areas in the second

[104] "Jokhang."

stage; the last four, the yang'dul, were built on the country's frontiers. The Jokhang temple was finally built in the heart of the srin ma, ensuring her subjugation.[105]

---

[105] Ibid.

16.7 Norbulingka:

In Tibetan, Norbulingka means Treasure Garden. or Treasure Park. The word "Lingka" is commonly used in Tibet to define all horticultural parks in Lhasa and other cities. When the Cultural Revolution began in 1966, Norbulingka was renamed People's Park and opened to the public. [106]

Norbulingka Palace of the Dalai Lamas was built about 100 years after the Potala Palace was built on the Parkori peak, over a 36 hectares 89 acres land area. It was built a little away to the west of the Potala for the exclusive use by the Dalai Lama to stay in during the summer months. Tenzing Gyatso, the present 14th Dalai Lama, stayed here before he fled to India. The building of the palace and the park was undertaken by the 7th Dalai Lama from 1755. The Norbulingka Park and Summer Palace were completed in 1783 under Jampel Gyatso, the 8th Dalai Lama, on the outskirts of Lhasa and became the summer residence during the reign of the Eighth Dalai Lama. [107]

---

[106] Wikipedia, "Norbulingka."
[107] Ibid.

Figure 19. Buddhist Temple

16.8 Drepung Monastery

'Drepung Monastery, located at the foot of Mount Gephel, is one of the "great three" Gelug University gompas (monasteries) of Tibet. The other two are Ganden Monastery and Sera Monastery.[108]

Drepung is the largest of all Tibetan monasteries and is located on the Gambo Utse Mountain, five kilometres from the western suburb of Lhasa.

Drepung Monastery was founded in 1416 by Jamyang Choge Tashi Palden (1397–1449), one of Tsongkhapa's main disciples, and it was named after the sacred abode in South India of Shridhanyakataka. Drepung was the principal seat of the Gelugpa school and it retained the premier place among the four great Gelugpa monasteries. The Ganden Phodrang (dga´ ldan pho brang) in Drepung was the residence of the Dalai Lamas until the Great Fifth Dalai Lama constructed the Potala. Drepung was known for the high standards of its academic

---

[108] Wikipedia, "Drepung Monastery."

study, and was called the Nalanda of Tibet, a reference to the great Buddhist monastic University of India. [109]

---

[109] Ibid.

17 Bibliography:

Alyaeva, Dinara. Director, Pomogat Legko, Russia.
"Annual Report of the Bureau of American Ethnology to the Secretary of the… Pdf." *Smithsonian Institution. Bureau of American Ethnology.*
Art, Rubin Museum of. "Bon Press Release."
BON RELIGION, CATHOLICS AND SUPERSTITION IN TIBET. "Bon Religion, Catholics and Superstition in Tibet."
buddhaweekly.com/. "I interview-Bon-Teacher-Chaphur-Rinpoche-Explains-Bon-Different-Similar-Five-Buddhist-Schools-Tibet."
Dictionary, Urban. "Shaman."
Drake, Michael. "Shamanic Drumming Shamanic Divination."
Eastburn, Drake. "Healer, Shaman, Facilitator." *International Journal of Complementary & Alternative Medicine* 5, no. 2 (2017).
Encyclopedia, Chinese Buddhist. "Shamanism in Mongolia and Tibet."
Ermakov, Dmitry. "Bo and Bon—Ancient Shamanic Traditions of Siberia and Tibet in Their Relation to the Teachings of a Central Asian Buddha."
GELFAND, MICHAEL. "Medicine and Magic." *The Central African Journal of Medicine.*
INDIAN, THE NATIONAL MUSEUM OF THE AMERICAN. "Do All Indians Live in Tipis?."
Jilek, Wolfgang G. "Transforming the Shaman Changing Western Views of Shamanism and Altered States of Consciousness."
Leore Grosman, Natalie D. Munro, and Anna Belfer-Cohen. "A 12,000-Year-Old Shaman Burial from the Southern Levant (Israel)."
Lin, Diana. "A Brief History of Tibet Autonomous Region." *Harvard University Graduate School of Education.*
Mumo, Peter M. "Holistic Healing, an Analytical Review of Medicine-Men in African Societies."
Peters, Larry G. "The 'Calling,' the Yeti, and the Ban Jhakri ('Forest Shaman') in Nepalese Shamanis."
Publishing, Kotan. "Mapping the Tibetan World."
Richard Noll, Kun Shi. "Chuonnasuan. The Last Shaman of the Oroqen of Ne China." *Journal of Korean Religions, 2004.*
Rinchen, Yönsiyebü. "White, Black and Yellow Shamans among the Mongols." *Ultimate Reality and Meaning* 4, no. 2 (1981): 94–102.
Sacredsites.com. "World Pilgrimigae Guide."
Sanders, Dr Fabian. "Tibetan Oracles and Himalayan Shamans."
Seminar, Tibetan Renaissance. "Bon Background Research from the Tibetan Renaissance Seminar."
shamanicdrumming.com. "Shamanic Drumming."
shamanlinks.net. "Singing Shamanic Songs—Shaman Links."
Tibet, Bon: Indigenous Shamanism of. "Bon—Indigenous Shamanism of Tibet."
warpaths2peacepipes.com. "Shaman."

Wikipedia. "Animism."
———. "Banjhakri and Banjhakrini."
———. "Drepung Monastery."
———. "Dzogchen."
———. "Ethnobotany."
———. "Jokhang."
———. "Medicine Bag."
———. "Medicine Man."
———. "Merit Buddhism."
———. "Mongolian Shamanism."
———. "Mount Kailash."
———. "Norbulingka."
———. "Paleolithic."
———. "Potala Palace."
———. "Prayer Flag."
———. "Psychopomp."
———. "Reincarnation.Pdf."
———. "Shamanism."
———. "Torma."
———. "Witch Doctor."
wingsofchaos.com. "Prologue for Zadkiel."